THE UPS AND DOWNS OF SAILING

THE UPS AND DOWNS OF SAILING

Richard Bishop

Book Guild Publishing

Sussex, England

First published in Great Britain in 2008 by
The Book Guild Ltd
Pavilion View
19 New Road
Brighton, BN1 1UF

Typesetting in Times by
Acorn Bookwork, Salisbury, Wiltshire

Printed in Great Britain by
CPI Antony Rowe

A catalogue record for this book is available from
The British Library.

ISBN 978 1 84624 262 5

Contents

List of Illustrations

LIST OF ILLUSTRATIONS

'My father spent most of my childhood trying
to drown me'
(Paul Bishop, Race Director of Sail Training
International)

'There are those who do, and there are those
who don't. Those who do make mistakes, and
learn by them. They go on to become good
sailors.'
(Alfred John Pengelly, 'J class' sailor, and well-
known West Country Fisherman)

Preface

A three-week summer holiday in Talland Bay in Cornwall in 1965 was a welcome break for my wife and me from teaching, organising holiday studies for French students, and of course coping with our three daughters, our son, and our dog 'Specks'. The obvious attractions of the West Country for a healthier outdoor life, and the possibility of sailing a family-sized boat, contrasted very favourably with our lives spent close to Heathrow Airport.

My best friend Trevor had already moved away from our area to work at Petter Marine, near Hamble. His entire family were enjoying a far better quality of life. He found time to join the works sailing club, which was based next to the old seaplane ramp, and he was having a great time.

He invited me to go sailing with him in one of the club's 'Jump Ahead' catamarans. Alas! Bad weather caused the sailing to be cancelled three times. However, on the last occasion the secretary said that as there were still two boats on the water, he would agree that a strong crew could take me for a spin.

Launching from the seaplane ramp into Southampton Water was exceedingly difficult, and three of us were soaked up to the armpits. One of the boats lost its rudders, and our boat was dismasted, after we had thrashed our way through some very rough water in near gale-force winds. This introduction to sailing, together with our Cornish holiday, inspired me to change the course of my family's life. Sailing was to become my great passion for many years.

1

My Own Interest in the Sea and Boats

My lifelong love affair with sailing all started when my father took my brother and me to Blackheath boating pond, to sail a three foot 'J Class' model yacht. I was only about four at the time, but I remember being fascinated by the wind making the model lean over as it gained speed. Someone, usually my brother, would have to run round to the other side of the pond, to stop it hitting the cement.

Two or three years later the whole family had a trip on a paddle steamer which I am sure should have been paid off in the Victorian times. Dad showed my brother and me how the great steam engines were at work turning the huge paddles. After the war we all went on another paddle steamer, which was a more modern one. I can recall being spellbound watching the river traffic, as we made our way to Margate.

Another cheaper trip on a paddle steamer was on the free Woolwich ferry, which we took to see Aunt Ada, who lived in one of the old worker's cottages, which backed onto the Royal Docks. Dad always took me to the large lock, close by. He always timed the visit so that we could see the great ships being nursed by the pier head staff and the tugs into the dock.

Years later Dad and I returned to the Royal Docks, to be shown over the *Pamir*, which was a full-rigged sailing vessel that had a more modern auxiliary engine. The ship was used for sail training and shipping cargo. Tragically this great ship was lost with all hands, and many of them were young cadets.

The *Llanstephan Castle* was one of the many liners, in which Dad served as a quartermaster. One day Dad came home from work and

1

had some exciting news. The liner was berthed in the Royal Docks, and he had been invited to visit her with his sons. What a great day it was, when he took us on his conducted tour, which brought his time on board back to life, and his great love of the sea was so apparent.

Another surprise followed when Dad persuaded a distant relative to take him and myself up the Thames as it delivered a string of barges. These were released in turn, into the care of a single lighterman, who had only a single long oar, or sweep, to direct his barge onto the mud berth with great precision. The cups of tea and sandwiches which Mother had provided, and Dad's running commentary, ended all too quickly, as we changed our mode of transport to a rattling tram for the return home.

My favourite times spent with Dad, who was in charge of docking the ships which went in and out of the Surrey commercial docks, were when he took me to work with him when I was on holiday. The pier head staff were good fun to be with, and had been exceptionally brave during the Second World War.

During the Blitz on the London docks, the staff endured continuous attacks by German bombers. On one of these raids the staff had to get an ammunition ship out of the docks and into the Thames, where it would not be a danger to the docks and the houses nearby if it was exploded by the bombers. During this operation the staff were constantly strafed and bombed. One of the bombs landed in the lock, blowing out the middle lock gates, as the men toiled to free the boat. Those men continued to work while the German fighters continued to machine-gun them.

For this remarkable bravery eight George Crosses were awarded to the pier head staff. Lots were drawn by the ten staff, but only eight of them were present on the lock at the time. Of the other two, one was in the bunker, and the other was absent because of illness. Under these circumstances, the King ordered his Prime Minister to award the medal of Valour to my father for his bravery. My brother and I still have the citations from Winston Churchill and the King.

Dad was only five feet six inches tall, but was very tall in stature in my eyes, and to those who worked with or knew him.

At the Age of Fifteen I Went to Sea on my Own

I hasten to add that it was only in a plywood canoe, whose watertight bulkheads leaked. I was staying with my friend Michel and his parents who lived in Le Havre in Normandy, for a four-week summer holiday. Most sunny days we spent at their beach chalet. It had its own wine cellar, a single canoe, and a double canvased canoe which was designed for surfing, and all these were put to good use.

However, one lunch time the family had important matters to attend to, so I was left to amuse myself for the afternoon on the beach. I spent some time looking at the rough seas breaking on the beach, and I decided that it was too rough for swimming, although I was a strong swimmer and Michel and I regularly swam quite long distances.

Eventually I reasoned that if I could launch the plywood canoe, and get beyond the surf without capsizing, I could have lots of fun riding the big waves. Once beyond the surf it dawned on me that the only safe way to get back ashore was to turn round and ride the surf back onto the beach.

However, unlike modern canoes which are water tight, this one would capsize and fill if caught broadside on one of the big waves. The sensible course was to keep paddling directly into the waves; until I reached the landfall buoy which was a considerable distance offshore, where I would make the turn close to the buoy. In the event of a capsize I could swim to the buoy, climb the ladder and wait to be rescued.

All went as planned, because I judged the turn perfectly, and I set off back to the beach, surfing in style. and riding the big breakers right up the sand, where a crowd had gathered, and ended up at the feet of Michel's parents, who gave me a good roasting for my stupidity.

3

It transpired that they had returned to the beach to find that their small canoe was missing. I was finally spotted heading towards England. They concluded that I had 'blown a gasket' and wanted to go home. Meanwhile Michel kept in the background and said nothing, remembering having taken me on a more hair-brained trip which had nearly cost us our lives.

My final act of folly was my dive from the top of the girder bridge, which spanned a disused dock where our swimming club was based. The very last time I had the opportunity to try out high diving was the last day of my holiday.

I finally plucked up courage and climbed the girders. An old lady in her black widow's weeds remonstrated with me for being so stupid. Not wanting to lose face. I launched myself into space, but misjudged the height, and hit the water vertically with such force that I did not arch my back. The water became darker and darker, as I headed towards the mud. I recovered some of my senses and began the long swim towards the light, with my lungs bursting, and strength failing. I surfaced only to find that I was surrounded by thick black oil. I still had to find a way clear of the oil towards a dockside ladder. I have never since been tempted to high dive again.

2

How I Learned to Sail My Smuggler's Yawl

'I'll do you a favour, Peter,' the Cornish fisherman said as he passed my friend a box of matches.

'You cheeky bugger! She will be proper 'ansome when we have finished with her,' Peter replied.

Thus started the restoration, on West Looe Quay in the summer of 1967, of my £60 worth of a two-man fishing lugger.

Morning Star was built in 1906 on the lines of a smuggler's boat for the local doctor in Polperro, because these boats had a reputation for being very fast. In 1911 the iron drop keel was removed, and a petrol/paraffin Kelvin Hughes marine engine was installed in its place. It was the first marine engine ever to be used in Polperro.

The hull below the waterline had been well preserved, with its annual coat of pitch, which was always applied on a hot summer's day, when all the boats were painted, and was an excuse for a social event. The top planks, or strakes, had been removed because of rot, so they were replaced and fastened to new half ribs. Thwarts, knees, gunwales, cappings, stem, foredeck, tiller, floor planks, engine box, cleats, outrigger, rudder, running and standing rigging, all had to be replaced or modified. The engine needed overhauling, and when I tried to start it I broke my finger. This no doubt pleased the retired old fishermen, who said that it would never work.

Finally my pride and joy was ready for launching, and was renamed *Charlotte* to change her luck. The gaggle of onlookers who were holding court on the quayside were neither enthusiastic nor encouraging about the restoration. 'That there engine will never

5

work, and the old girl will never see the Eddystone again,' was their considered verdict.

Now it was time to learn the art of 'no frills' sailing from my friend Peter. Handling dipping lugsails, using moveable ballast, reading the weather, understanding the vagueness of the sea, navigation without aids, getting to know my own backyard, and nautical terms, all these and many more had to be mastered before I could safely sail over the horizon on my own.

The Yawl Dipping Lugsail Rig

The mizzen mast was off-set to allow the long tiller to move. The long outrigger was unshipped in harbour. The mizzen sail's halyard and sheet were fastened on cleats.

The mainmast had three stays fixed at the mast head; two of them were fixed to chain plates, and one to the stem. The inconvenience of this rig when tacking calls for the sheet to be slackened off, and the down haul, which is fixed to the bottom forward corner of the sail, must be released. Pulling the front of the sail down will lift the yardarm enough for it to be dipped and pushed round to the other side of the mast. The sail can now be reset for the opposite tack. The mizzen lugsail is dipped in the same manner. Reefing points are found on the mainsail but I rarely used them. The mizzen lugsail is dipped in the same manner.

Small boxes placed on either sides of the boat were used to store half-hundredweight weights, which were used to help keep the boat upright in strong winds.

The hull, being all in the water, managed to sail tolerably well to windward, although it was poor by comparison with modern yachts.

Charlotte, unlike most women, proved to be easily handled, although very fast. She gave lots of pleasure, excitement, and was pleasing to the eye.

My family's move from the Heathrow area proved to be very worthwhile, because I enjoyed teaching in a small secondary school

Figure 1   *Charlotte*, 18′6″ OA dipping lugsail yawl. Looe 1967.

Temporary Bowsprit & Trysail
for Race to Salcombe

Figure 2   Dipping lugsail yawl rig. *Charlotte*, 1906. Engine fitted 1911.

which had a real family atmosphere, and the outdoor life was so much healthier for us all. Specks, our dog, was in his element chasing the local bitches; and scrounging titbits from the tourists. *Charlotte*, my family and I, had never looked so healthy.

Most of the trips and cruises, which I now recount have depended on others, whose company and support I appreciate.

No Turning Back

The first opportunity Peter and I had to put *Charlotte* through her paces, a very large swell had been caused by a storm in the Atlantic, which had kept the fishing fleet firmly tethered to dry land. However, we both decided that it would be quite safe to sail in the shelter of Looe Island. Unfortunately we were carried away by our enthusiasm, excitement, and the bad conditions which we found some four miles or so from the harbour.

Peter shouted, 'We will never make it back to the harbour, so we must run downwind to find shelter in Plymouth.' We made a hair-raising dash through very rough seas and big swells, to reach calm waters at Cawsand. It had been my first experience of such bad conditions, and rounding Rame Head at close quarters was quite frightening for a novice, especially with the waves trying to mount the cliffs so near us.

Hours later, when the wind seemed to have abated and we had dried out, we foolishly tried to sail home. Poking our bows out from our refuge, and heading into the open sea, we punched our way through three waves, and had shipped a lot of water. We had no choice but to join the other boats seeking shelter from the gale in Sutton Harbour. As we raced across Plymouth Sound we savoured the prospect of a hot drink on dry land, and a chauffeured car to take us home. I was no longer scared stiff.

Charlotte proved to be very fast and seaworthy, and I looked forward to serving my apprenticeship aboard her. She had turned out to be more of a boat than I was a seaman.

A few days later I collected *Charlotte*, and set off back home. My initial course was to pass the western end of the breakwater. Much to my surprise, HMS *Ocean* was on a converging course with mine, but I held on for a while. I was even more surprised to see one of the navigators use his Aldis lamp to inform me that his vessel was about to turn to starboard. Naturally I got out of his way as he commanded a slightly larger vessel than mine! However, I wondered if he was obliged to signal me or it was just his sense of humour.

A Sense of Direction

I had been determined to visit the Eddystone lighthouse at my first opportunity, but when the chance arrived the visibility was down to a quarter of a mile, and I had yet to buy a compass and a chart.

I fixed my course by selecting two leading marks, which I had chosen from my four-inch-to-the-mile map, which pointed in the right direction. I set off on my own, following these marks until they disappeared, and by this time I had observed our angle of approach to the waves so I kept going. I also kept an eye on the sunlight which was stronger in one direction. Nevertheless, I wondered if and when I would see the lighthouse, or whether I would land up in Brittany.

Eventually, and to my relief, the target appeared dead ahead through the mist. Then the fishing fleet appeared, making its way back to port. The leading boat came alongside me and its young skipper, my friend Peter's son, called out, 'What the hell are you doing out here? You better follow us before you get lost.' This I did with my tail between my legs, and I counted my error of judgement as useful experience.

The very next day I bought a chart and a compass.

Portwrinkle and the Whale or Shark?

Peter suggested that we should sail along the coast towards Whitsand Bay, to see if it was possible to enter the remains of Portwrinkle harbour, which was totally destroyed in a violent storm many generations ago. To his knowledge no sailing vessels had been there since. The downside was that there was no trace of any leading marks to guide us through the reefs and the remains of the sunken ruins of the harbour walls.

Patrick, one of Peter's wilder friends, joined us for our little adventure. En route we spotted a basking shark of over twenty-five feet in length, idling its way up channel. Patrick grabbed the boat hook, leapt onto the foredeck and pretended to harpoon it. Peter swung the helm to port and aimed *Charlotte* at the monster. I slammed the engine into reverse just in time to avoid a very dodgy outcome of my crew's sense of humour.

Shortly afterwards we carefully approached the reefs, and some how missed them, more by good luck than judgement. We then glided over the remains of the harbour wall with only inches to spare. We then knew where to look for the leading marks, and found two small stone boxes set in the cliff where lanterns were put many years ago.

We made our way to the public bar at the Whitsand Bay Hotel for a drink. However, the dress code for the evening was 'evening dress de rigeuer'. Our embarrassment rather spoiled the taste of our beer, but we stood our ground and ignored the disapproving looks the other customers gave us for being in jeans. Negotiating our way out to sea safely was straightforward, and we set sail back home.

When we arrived at the Banjo Pier it was crowded with summer visitors enjoying the balmy night air. Patrick jumped up onto the foredeck and, mimicking a German accent, called out, 'Is dis England?' as we swept past on the flood tide. Several onlookers replied, 'This is Looe.' 'Vas ist Looe,' Peter said, shrugging his shoulders. Several obliging young men ran along the pier, trying in vain to catch up with us to explain. The contrast of the chaos caused by Patrick's sense of humour and the tranquillity of the scene was amazing. Very angry anglers whose rods, lines and gear were being towed upstream faster than the young men could run made us laugh, especially when they realised it was a leg pull!

Free Timber

One evening after school Peter asked me if he could borrow *Charlotte* and myself for a few hours. He told me that a timber ship had jettisoned its deck cargo of timber to avoid the ship capsizing in the rough seas and gale-force winds. All that free timber just waiting to be collected encouraged us to overload *Charlotte* so much that there remained little free space. The only place left for us to stand was on top of our large stack of timber. We contemplated jettisoning some of our ill-gotten gains, because we could capsize in the rough seas with so little freeboard.

Without any warning a very large basking shark dived beneath our midships leaving a hole in the water just like a submarine does when it dives.

The price of our greed could well have been fatal. Once ashore we soon offloaded our loot, and Peter disappeared with it in his van before customs and excise arrived, as is the tradition amongst Cornish folk.

A Sunday lunch time pint in Polperro

Some weeks later Peter, his friend and I left Looe for a pint or two in Polperro. Because the wind was NE Force 7, I preferred to use the Kelvin Hughes engine plus a 4-horsepower (HP) outboard, instead of sailing, so I unshipped the rudder. Keeping in the lee of the cliffs, we soon arrived at our destination, where we enjoyed our beer.

On leaving the harbour we spotted the young skipper (the son of

11

Peter the boat builder) who had choked me off for sailing to the Eddystone Lighthouse without a compass, and in very poor visibility. We offered him a lift as we would be passing Talland. where he lived. 'Not bloody likely,' was his reply, as he glanced skywards at the menacing clouds and then at the sea which was rough, even close inshore. Of course he had good sense, as we were about to find out.

We shipped a lot of water, and the spray was so violent we had to divert it away from the helmsman's face, in order for him to see where we were going. We hugged the coast as close as possible to find some shelter, but the gale became stronger, and the bilge water needed to be pumped out all the time.

Rounding the headland at Hannafore, more water came into the boat than we could pump out, and the bilge water was sloshing from gunwale to gunwale. Approaching the Banjo Pier directly gave us some respite from the wind, but as I steered with the outboard, it came adrift, leaving us rudderless, and going straight towards the pier. The main engine was put into reverse, just in time to slow down enough for us to ram the pier very gently.

The humourist in the crew said, 'I can see the headlines in the *Cornish Times* tomorrow – FISHING BOAT RAMS AND SINKS BANJO PIER – 50 DROWN.'

3

Three Homepride Flour Graders and Three Broken Ribs

The forecast NW Force 6–7 wind seemed a little strong for the day trip that Peter Astin, his friend and I had planned to Salcombe for a quick pint and sandwich before returning home before dark. I had rigged a temporary bowsprit, using an old trysail as jib to give some extra speed. With all three sails polled out we made a very fast crossing to the Mew Stone at Wembury Bay. Then, with a strengthening wind, *Charlotte* climbed up on the plane, and remained there thundering towards Bolt Head. Finally we turned towards Salcombe, at a less exhilarating speed of about seven knots!

On our arrival we were greeted by the harbourmaster, who called out, 'Who the hell gave you permission to come up here from Looe?' 'You will be staying of course, and are welcome to a free mooring of your choice,' was his kind offer!

When I told him that we had only called in for a pint, he looked up at the scudding clouds. He wished us a safe return. 'But of course they have real sailors in Looe,' he said in a loud voice to the bystanders. At one time he had been the harbourmaster in Looe, so perhaps he was a little biased.

The weather was closing in, so we reluctantly hurried our lunch and set off, not relishing the prospect of a long, hard and wet beat to windward. We had barely set off when a brutal squall hit us, and forced us to lie a hull for over an hour. We drifted further and further from the shelter of land. Slowly we plucked up courage to get moving. Under reefed main lugsail and mizzen-lugsail, and with engine running, we set course towards Bolt Tail. As we drew nearer

13

I could see the breaking seas trying to climb the cliffs. The closer we got to Bolt Tail the more I realised that we could not safely make our way back against gale-force winds and seas. Our best bet was to try and make it to Burgh Island, where I could put the crew ashore. It was a slow, wet journey, with many an anxious moment en route. Dropping the lads off as planned, I then had to motor in towards the mouth of the River Avon, with the surf close by on either side, higher than the gunwales, but we made it to the sharp right turn under the cliff. In an instant, *Charlotte* shot into the tranquility of the river, where I left her anchored up for the night. It turned out to be a good decision. We were able to return to the comfort and safety of our own homes for the night.

The forecast for the next day was again NW Force 7. We returned to the river Avon hoping for an easier ride, bringing with us a 4HP outboard, to assist the boat's ancient engine push our way to windward faster. Keeping close inshore we made relatively good progress, until we started to cross Plymouth Sound, which was open to the full force of the gale, and being wind against tide, caused a disturbed and rough sea. Shortly afterwards and without any warning, three loud cracking sounds came in quick succession. These were  made by the snapping of three ribs – two starboard and one port – breaking. Being a carvel hull, the ribs hold the planks together, and with three of the ribs broken others might follow suit. I feared for the survival of *Charlotte* and ourselves. The only safe decision I could think of was to move forward slowly in the calmer water between the waves. It took an eternity of nail-biting concentration to ease our way to Rame Head, where at last we dropped anchor in calm water. It was now safe to stand up, stretch our legs and breathe normally. What a sight we made – we were all completely covered in thick salt except for our eyes and mouths, resembling three Home Pride Flour Graders dipped in flour!

Our passage continued along the coast, keeping within swimming distance of the land as far as possible, until we reached Looe.

14

Figure 3   Looe Harbour, East Quay.

Home at last, but with memories etched boldly in our minds of our lucky escape, to be recounted in the comfort of a fireside during a winter storm, or resulting in nightmares about the sound of cracking wood.

Alas poor *Charlotte* was no longer fit to sail, so I had to give serious consideration about her future. On one hand she deserved to join the other craft at the Exeter Boat Museum, but on the other hand, with a major refit and conversion, she might be suitable for cruising. The bottom line was I lacked the finance to replace her with a four-berth sea-going sloop, for my planned cruise to the Channel Islands, the Normandy Coast and Dorset. I estimated that, with hard work, it was possible to repair and convert her for the following season's adventures.

Winter Refit and Conversion

I purchased an ancient Ford Prefect to use as a mobile workshop, then I set to work replacing all of the ribs, making sure that the hull

15

was sound and seaworthy. With help from my son and Peter Green-wood, I started on the conversion. We were fortunate to receive donations of a Redwing mast, boom and sails, together with Mirror sails and many other valuable gifts of timber and plywood which came from unexpected sources. Advice and encouragement from friends, well-wishers and onlookers kept me going through the cold winter days spent on the wind swept East Looe Quay. Even my long-suffering dog Specks found it hard going, and he would leave his job of watching *Charlotte* metamorphosing into a Bermudan yawl, to run home to warmth and comfort. Finally spring came, and the old lady had been face-lifted, and was ready to be craned into the water.

Launching is always a worry because it doesn't always go according to plan, as I once witnessed when a ship was being launched into the Tyne. The wind blew the ship against a tower

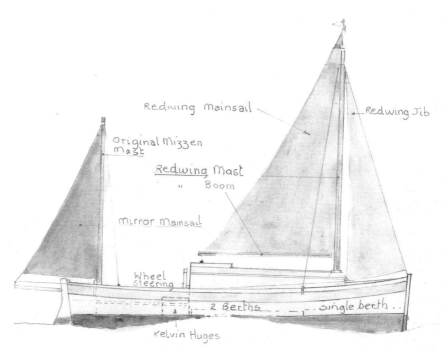

Figure 4 Sketch from memory of *Charlotte*'s new cabin and rig made from donated parts and materials.

Figure 5   Gaff-rigged working boats at Forder Creek, Saltash.

Figure 6   *Espinet 2*'s winter mooring (on left-hand side).

crane, as it left the slipway. The crane driver came down his ladder as though he was in freefall.

However, *Charlotte* settled gracefully on the water, and did not sink. I was now the proud owner of a half decker, with a three-berth cabin which boasted a head height for dwarfs, wheel steering, bucket heads, and even new white plastic fenders, instead of worn-out car tyres. I was very pleased to contemplate sleeping on a bunk instead of trying to sleep under a lugsail, dew drenched and stiff from lying on wet floorboards.

My plans for sleepovers at the head of the Tamar and Helford Rivers would now be in four-star accommodation, compared with the last head-of-river trip that my son and I made to Lostwithiel on the Fowey River.

The village got its name when nearly all the fishermen drowned in a hellish storm. I spent a restless night feeling the unease of the ghostly fishermen.

4

Nearly Neaped at Gweek

In preparation for our summer cruise, Ewart Sturrock, a colleague and close friend and I decided to sail down to Mounts Bay, via the head of the Helford River, to Gweek. We set course directly for the mouth of the Helford in very poor visibility. This was going to stretch my navigational skills to the limit, because a compass and chart were my only aids.

Much to our amazement we sailed into the Helford estuary without seeing anything other than mist and sea. Relaxed and reassured by the sight of land, we ambled upstream to Gweek, where we enjoyed a pleasant visit to the local pub. We were feeling rather smug with our navigation and seamanship, until the landlord asked where we planned to moor up for the night. I told him we expected to leave soon.

'If you leave her where she is, she will be neaped. The tide is on the turn and you will be very lucky to find deeper water downstream in the dark,' he said. Panic set in as we rushed to get going, only to find that it was pitch dark.

At first the river was narrow, and with the aid of a good torch we could make out the river banks; as we slowly crept downstream. The river widened and became so shallow we touched the bottom all the time, as we groped around trying to find midstream. I had the bright idea of hauling our Calor gas lantern up to the top of the main mast, to illuminate the darkness, but it got stuck and became a serious hazard instead. As it swung to and fro, with our attempts to dislodge it, a flight of helicopters approached. Had someone raised the alarm thinking we were signalling our distress? No. The helicopters, which were flying very low, continued on their way, their down-draught making the lamp gyrate even more dangerously.

Lady Luck was with us briefly, as the lantern decided to unravel itself from the halyard, and we stumbled upon the midstream gravel. We anchored downstream exhausted, and brewed up the finest cup of tea, which tasted like nectar. We woke at first light to find Lady Luck had just had enough of us for one day. *Charlotte* had come to rest on the edge of a very steep mud bank, leaning badly and her bows pointing skywards. Mudflats and no signs of life, and the with the likelihood of us capsizing, all was pure gloom and doom.

The only way we could prevent the boat from being swamped by the incoming tide was to pass a rope round a partly submerged tree trunk, and winch Charlotte more upright. A good idea, but the trunk was too far away, and it was too dangerous to leave the boat. A boat hook, some floorboards, and a mud bath solved the problem. It took ages to clean up the mud which had somehow spread throughout the boat, and from our heads to our feet.

In poor visibility and a moderate wind, we completed our passage to Newlyn, with only a glimpse of the Lizard Lighthouse en route to establish our position. On our arrival at 1 a.m., a uniformed figure was standing on the quayside to greet us. He demanded to know how we had managed to arrive without 'them' knowing. He also wanted to know how many there were on board, and why we had come to Newlyn. This customs officer was very doubtful as to our bona fide status, and I am sure that marked our card for surveillance. Perhaps he thought that I was a people smuggler, and I had a dozen or so concealed on board! Next morning, it dawned on me that we were running out of time, and we would have to beat to windward in rough seas to clear Mounts Bay if we had any hope of getting back in time for work.

With Ewart at the helm we set off in poor visibility, strengthening wind and a choppy sea. With his eyes glued to the compass he maintained his course, whilst I kept watch. Gradually the waves and wind seemed to change their direction and we were now going back to Newlyn. This was my first experience of a magnetic disturbance phenomenon which had not been caused by iron objects being near the compass. At the same time the wind increased, and I began to doubt the wisdom of pressing on. However, with the assistance of our ancient engine, we made for Porthleven until the engine died.

Quickly I shipped the 4HP outboard. With Ewart still at the helm, I tried to resuscitate the engine, but I found it was a hopeless task, as sea water had turned the oil in the exhaust into emulsion. We came to within a mile of the harbour, but were unable to force our way any further because of the gale. The outboard finally spluttered to a halt because it had used up the last drop of petrol.

As the anchor was unlikely to hold under the conditions, I regretfully decided to return to Newlyn under storm headsail. Sitting on the foredeck and trying to set it, was like sitting on a bucking bronco at a rodeo and changing your shirt at the same time! We were making about 5 knots downwind towards Newlyn in very poor visibility when the sea suddenly became very angry, and collapsed in fury, great noise, and dense spray. We were thrown all over the place.

There was little choice but to continue on our way, on the roller-coaster ride towards Newlyn, but my constant fear was to miss our target and get caught on a leeshore. However, the harbour did appear through the mist directly in front of us, as we were being battered by large waves which threatened to smash us against the harbour wall. A group of hardy onlookers, eager for some excitement, were getting soaked by the spray that was coming over the sea wall. They were not disappointed as they watched a large breaking sea surf us, bows down through the entrance, with little room to spare between the breaking seas on either side of us.

Adrenaline-saturated and sea-soaked, we came alongside a trawler. *Charlotte* remained in harbour like an abandoned puppy, whilst we travelled home in comfort by train, still shell-shocked by our experiences, in particular the moment we crossed the Welloe, which is where conflicting tidal currents meet.

The next weekend, with the prospect of moderate conditions and good visibility, we made a dash to Newlyn to bring the boat back to Looe. It would also give us a chance of seeing where we had been, and where we were going for a change.

By the time we reached Coverack it was already dark and the conditions became more lively. It took longer than I had anticipated for us to round the Lizard, and safely pass the Manacles. As we were making our way to Dodman Point we nearly ran down a little red light which was bobbing up and down in the waves, and a few minutes later we saw some unfamiliar navigation lights, which moved at great speed. Ewart shone the torch on the red mainsail to warn of our presence, but only just in time. A helicopter came straight towards us, and hovered so close that our torch illuminated the pilot's face. He obviously mistook the glow of our torch on the sail for the red light on the antisubmarine device which was to be retrieved. We had just avoided a fatal accident by having a mast slightly shorter that his height above the water.

Anchoring in the outer harbour at Mevagissey, we slept for the remainder of the night. Next morning I was met by some glorious sunshine and a customs officer seated in his official mini, observing us. We had been marked down for surveillance. After a relaxed breakfast and numerous cups of tea, we set sail, and thoroughly enjoyed the last leg of our adventure. Back at school the next day, I wondered how Ewart would describe our mishaps. Many years later he told me that it had been one the most memorable events in his life. Good or bad though, that is the question!

5

The Summer Cruise 1971

Preparation for the cruise entailed working in a burger bar for four weeks to finance it. Even so, I could afford to spend very little on equipment, and this included the inflatable dinghy, radio direction finder and a log. The tidal atlas, chart and the pilot guide were essential, as was the availability of two suitable crew members.

Ewart was only free for two weeks, but I was pleased to accept his offer. Paul, my 14-year-old son, had already become a competent young sailor, and a great companion, so I was delighted he wanted to sail with us. We decided to sail up the River Dart to Totnes, before crossing the Channel to Alderney, then on to Cherbourg, back over to Weymouth, Brixham and back to Looe. Waiting impatiently slaving over a hot griddle was the hardest part of my preparations.

The last beefburger had been cooked and our stores were on board, so we set sail for foreign shores with enthusiasm and optimism, but without much cash. It was a fine sunny day, we had a fair wind, and the outlook was very good. Indeed, the first day's passage turned out to be quite idyllic!

Peter, the boat builder, was waiting for us on the quayside at Dartmouth, and all four of us set off to enjoy the delights of sailing the old lady *Charlotte* through the tranquil Devon countryside to Totnes. Our return journey was very relaxed, and as we drifted downstream, a gentle ebb tide helped us on our way. The wind barely filled the sails, and the balmy air did little to brace us for the passage ahead.

The evening meal at a nearby restaurant rounded off a very nice

23

day, spent in good company. We returned to the boat to find that she had come to rest on a huge boulder at low tide. It had pushed two of her planks inward, making the hull non-watertight. I feared the worst! Peter, in his usual laid-back manner, said, 'I'll soon put her to rights, if you've got a block of wood and a heavy hammer.' After some violent thumping, the carvel planks sprang back into place. He assured me that the hull was watertight again. Peter's work was well done, thank goodness. He looked very wistful as he stood on the quayside waving us goodbye, as we set sail for the other side. No doubt he wished he was coming with us.

Conditions were good for the crossing, but the light wind made for slow progress. Gradually the wind strengthened and the visibility began to fall. It was nice to pick up speed, but I had banked on making our landfall in good visibility. Lacking a log, and relying on my 'guestimates' of speed through the water, made my navigation a rather hit-or-miss affair.

It would now be essential to pick up the correct foghorn signal. The closer we approached the land, the stronger the wind became, the denser the mist became, and the harder it was to locate where the foghorn signal came from.

Suddenly a lighthouse appeared, which was surely the right one, but we were far too close to the rocks. Quickly we turned and followed the coast westwards on a strong tidal flow. It was with help from the engine that we were able to stem the tide and reach the safety of the outer harbour.

The delights of shore leave eluded us as we had no dinghy, and no one fancied climbing the very tall and vertiginous ladder. But needs must and Muggins set off to find a dinghy for hire. Alas! The only thing for hire that floated was a double canoe whose 'watertight' bulkheads both leaked.

Ferrying Ewart and Paul called for nerves of steel and good judgement, because both craft were bobbing up and down on different wave lengths. All three of us enjoyed our time ashore and the luxury of walking more than a few feet at a time, although the ground felt like rubber, but we didn't need to hold on to something all the time, even after we had downed a few glasses of ale. However, the cost of accommodation and food which was cooked on more than one small Calor gas stove was beyond our budgets.

We returned to the canoe and braced ourselves for the game of Russian roulette, where the loser falls overboard. After two nights of being shaken and stirred by the swell and the wind and drenched by the spray, I felt like one of James Bond's cocktails.

The harbourmaster had already visited all craft in the outer harbour. He instructed all skippers to lay out all the anchor chain they had, in order to keep their boats safe in the gale. One of the skippers didn't heed the warning, and sure enough his expensive yacht tripped its anchor. He was shouting and panicking big time as his pride and joy headed for the rocks. Holding the mizzen sail at an angle, *Charlotte* swung towards the doomed yacht. We managed to hold it alongside until the skipper let out more chain on our instructions. I was very disappointed he couldn't even thank us for our timely help in saving his yacht.

The following morning the conditions had improved somewhat, so I decided to make a dash for Cherbourg, instead of enduring another night of purgatory. The harbourmaster did warn me that we might not make our destination because the very strong foul tide might start before we had passed Cap de la Hague. Foolishly my optimism overcame my common sense, and with a Force 7 favourable wind to help us on our way, we set sail for Cherbourg.

Near Cap de la Hague, we were still doing seven knots, but leading marks confirmed that we were going backwards. Ewart refused to believe this, seeing our powerful bow wave and wash. My only sensible choice was to run down the Cherbourg peninsula to the first harbour. The land flashed by as we raced for shelter at Dielette, at a combined speed of 16 to 17 knots!

We enjoyed a good meal, and had our best night's sleep since leaving Devon.

Early next morning we joined the local fishermen in their local bar for our breakfast of Calvados, coffee and croissants. The smell of alcoholic fumes, Gauloises smoke, garlic, fish and old oilies takes a lot of beating for local colour. Walking with fresh air in our lungs along the harbour wall towards *Charlotte*, we were overtaken by two gendarmes on motorcycles. They were looking for us no doubt. Someone had reported three suspicious-looking characters sneaking into their harbour without showing the yellow flag or flying the French flag. Seeing *Charlotte* they must have decided that she couldn't have been out in such rough weather.

We made a hasty departure for Cherbourg. Under full sail, and with help from a strong wind, we made a quick passage round the Cap de la Hague. Shortly afterwards I noticed that we were gradually sinking lower into the water. Suddenly, two jets of high-pressure water shot skywards from the stem. Commonsense prevailed and, we slowed down, releasing both sheets just in time to prevent us from being driven under, and no doubt drowning in the process. Ewart  and I gave Paul the honour to taking the helm for the rest of the journey. 'Well done, First Mate!'

The bad weather continued, leaving us pottering about on a very meagre budget, moored up alongside expensive yachts, and looking like their down-and-out relations. Ewart's first priority was to let his wife know that he might be late getting home. My own telephone call home was overdue, so we all three set off to find a public call box. But there weren't any and the bar owners wouldn't let us make an international call. One of them explained that we would have to go to the central post office, and book the call.

Arriving at the main concourse of the PTT (the French post office), we found a long straggling queue made up of all sorts of sizes and colours of local people, not forgetting the numerous widows dressed in black. The conglomeration of bicycles, pushchairs, live rabbits and chickens ready for the pot, parcels and paraphernalia bought at the market was being moved forward slowly by the owners.

At the head of the shambles an overbearing and dour spinster was perched high above her subjects, seated behind a tall pedestal-style desk. Her job was to direct the callers to a vacant cabin once their connection had been made. At last our turn came. 'Well, what do want?' the old crone demanded. 'I would like to make a call to Looe please,' I replied in French. Her face turned crimson and she started to stutter, 'How dare you.' 'I must telephone Looe in Cornwall, England.' I insisted 'Well what is Looe then?' she said. I repeated my request to the laughter and giggles from the waiting crowd. Goaded by her embarrassment, and my insistence, she contacted the international exchange in Paris and relayed my request. There followed a heated argument and the man on the other end of the line refused to comply. 'Give me your handset and I will tell him myself,' I told her. This she did. The crowd were giving their opinion of me, the British, and my rudeness. My further explanation as  to where and what Looe was resulted in us getting our cabin number, and the urgent connection home.

It turns out that 'Looe' in French means a house of convenience – a toilet or brothel. My French did eventually improve after I spent ten years of my retirement in the south of France, the happiest time of my life.

Frustrated by our lack of time and money, we decided to make a dash for Weymouth, in what I thought would be a Force 7 westerly. Having made five miles or so in what was obviously a full-bodied gale, I decided to turn back and we battled our way back, getting wetter all the time. It was impossible to make ground to windward, because of the very strong west-to-east tidal flow. At one stage it looked as though we would be swept past the eastern entrance. I was dry mouthed, and very apprehensive about the outcome.

Luck was with us, and we managed to return to our previous berth, washed out and tired. We set to clearing up and pumping out. Word soon spread that we had ventured out in the gale, and this soon had our neighbours looking at *Charlotte* and her crew with less disdain. That evening we three set off to find a good vantage spot, so that we could weigh up the weather, the conditions in the harbour and in the open sea. As we walked through a waterside site which had been bulldozed ready for redevelopment, a police car stopped beside us. The senior policeman grilled me with question after question, which made me feel very uncomfortable. 'Who are you? What are you lot doing in this isolated place? Why have you come to Cherbourg?' I did my best to answer his questions, and I began to understand why he had followed us. Someone must have suggested that Ewart and I were paedophiles, and Paul the victim. Having satisfied my inquisitors, they drove away laughing like drainpipes at my embarrassment and their mistake.

In the morning the forecast for Southampton was Gale 8 westerly, and in my opinion the weather system was moving up the Channel. All being well it would leave us with more moderate winds in its wake. Ewart was very anxious to get home, so it was 'all systems go'.

With all sails set, and a strong wind on our port beam, *Charlotte* was at her very best, riding the impressive swell and brushing aside the waves. The only boat we saw on the crossing was a large oceangoing yacht, coming up channel under spinnaker. We were constantly dropping our of their sight because of the deep troughs, and no doubt the crew were curious about the strange little craft which kept bobbing up and down like a nodding man.

Our visitors caught up with us, and rounded our stern, a manoeuvre done when we were on the crest of a wave and on the peak of the swell. We looked down on the yacht, as the crew lined the rail, out of respect for us. It was a complete surprise, which we appreciated. As night fell, I went below to relax in the Spartan comfort of the cabin and was kidding myself that everything was going along swimmingly.

Sitting on my bunk with my feet on the opposite one, I felt the hull was being squeezed by the waves, and at the same time some organ music was being played on the radio. The image of Captain Nemo descending 20,000 leagues under the sea flashed through my mind, and I imagined *Charlotte*'s hull falling apart and us sharing his fate.

Ewart was still on tenterhooks about getting back on time, so I decided to drop him off in Portland harbour next to the road, so he could start hitchhiking straight away. All went well and he made his deadline. Paul and I continued on to Weymouth for supplies, and a well-deserved rest. We got our heads down very early in preparation for our appointment at the crack of dawn, with the Portland race, which is caused by the meeting of the tides between the Bill and the Shambles sandbank.

Having chosen the quietest time to go through the race, I was surprised that we were still shaken and stirred more than I expected. At last we found calm waters and sunshine, which was a wonderful change from all the bad weather we had put up with since Alderney.

Halfway across the bay towards Brixham, our next port of call. Paul went below to brew a cup of tea to celebrate our good fortune. 'There is a hell of a lot of water in here,' he shouted. Indeed the water was above the floorboards, and our nearest dry land was 15 miles away! Panic! Pumping, and bailing out did not lower the level 'Throw the ballast over the side,' I shouted, as I pumped hard enough to burst a vein. The Portland race had had the last word by causing a plank to come away from the stem. With the loss of ballast, and  our frantic efforts, we managed to get the leaking plank above the sea level. Unable to find a suitable berth, we anchored, and spent the night pumping. Next day we dried out alongside where I repaired the fault with a couple of copper nails and a hammer.

Once we had left Berry Head it was all downhill sailing, sunshine, relaxation and time to soak up the scenery and to contemplate.

Charlotte had turned out to be a wonderful investment. The sixty pounds had provided my friends, family and colleagues and some pupils with the chance to fish, adventure and visit the hidden gems of the Devon and Cornish coasts which are only accessible in a seagoing boat. I had also gained valuable experience by pushing my luck.

One of the old-timers summed me up: 'That silly bugger only goes out sailing when it's a least a half a gale.' Partly true! But there were countless trips in fine weather that were trouble free.

I remember returning home from Falmouth, when the sea was perfectly flat as far as the eye could see, and it had the colour of polished gold. Floating objects appeared to be suspended in a timeless space, filled with a golden mist. For over an hour *Charlotte* glided through the stillness of another dimension, which the great artist Turner could not replicate.

On another occasion I saw a breathtaking crystal green sky. The odds of seeing one is twice in a lifetime spent in the South West, looking in the right direction.

6

What's Next?

Up to this stage, only Paul, my oldest daughter Gillian and I had enjoyed being on board *Charlotte*. Perhaps my wife and my two other daughters, Kim and Beverley, would feel safer in a larger, more family-friendly boat than poor old *Charlotte*, with her spartan comforts. I was determined to acquire a four-berth sea-going yacht eventually.

However, my sailing career was to be shaped by the Cornwall Education Committee's decision to promote sailing in its secondary schools, because of the outstanding traditions of seafaring in Cornwall. Transport by sea and waterways was the only reliable method of transport, as the roads were impassable during the winter. Trade with the city of Brest far surpassed trade with London, and at one time the main language was French. Even the taxes paid for the construction of the impressive castle in Brest.

Teachers already involved in teaching sailing like myself were invited to attend a residential course at Falmouth, which was organised by the national sailing coach, on behalf of the Royal Yachting Association. One day he asked if anyone could suggest where he could obtain an anchor, as he needed to use one for a demonstration. It just happened that I had driven to Falmouth in my ancient Ford Prefect, or rather my mobile workshop, as my wife was using the family car to go to work. 'I have one in my car,' I said, to which he replied, 'Don't your brakes work?' Humour was just one of the ingredients of our outstanding course.

Everyone was expected to instruct novices and experienced sailors in a variety of day boats. In addition we had an opportunity to demonstrate our skills in handling larger vessels. My own first 'tipping point' came when I was instructing an experienced female (experienced in the art of sailing, of course) on how to handle a day boat in the confines of a dock. She mistimed a tack and nearly caused the masthead to get jammed under the quay decking. I touched the tiller and she let go. I slewed the boat clear of danger just in time. 'Next time, start to tack earlier,' I said.

The final part of the course was an oral examination, which was held at the Royal Cornwall Yacht Club. My examiner seemed satisfied with my answers, until he came to ask me how I would set up a dinghy race for a group of 14- to 16-year old school pupils. With one rescue boat to tend twelve boats, assuming the same conditions and venue that I could see in front of me.

'I am surprised you have even suggested the idea,' I said. 'The wind is already Force Seven, and one rescue boat could not cope with all the possible capsizes.' He did his very best to make me change my mind, and he became very curt at my obstinacy, and finally said, 'Well, you had better go now.' The outcome of our dual of words was that I was awarded the National School Sailing Master's and Senior RYA Instructor's Certificates.

One of the group suggested that I should join the Ocean Youth Club, as it was doing such a good job providing opportunities for youngsters, especially deprived ones. The club's boat, the *Falmouth Packet*, was based in Plymouth, where examinations for skipper and first mate's tickets were being held later on. I decided to find out more about the organisation.

The Ocean Youth Club

My introduction to the OYC turned out to be a baptism of fire, when I turned up for my first mate's ticket at Millbay dock. It was a Friday, which was the change-over day, so there were two crews, and inspiring candidates all milling about on board the *Falmouth Packet*.

I was instructed to prepare the boat for sea, and then to take her out into Plymouth Sound as quickly as possible. My protest that I needed time to sort out the crew's jobs, as well as familiarise myself with the chart and so on, was brushed aside. I was told to get moving. Willing hands set to, and off we set on a course which I was not familiar with. Naturally I told the examiner that I was not happy about this if I was supposed to be in charge of the boat at this stage.

I was then directed to change course, which would bring us very close to the western end of the breakwater. Nevertheless, I was pleased with the set of the sails, and we were making good progress to windward.

Figure 7   The dunking!

Figure 8   Near the top of the main mast.

33

'How do you know that we will clear the breakwater safely?' the examiner asked.

'Look behind and you will see our true course by the direction of our wake,' I replied.

My experience in handling my own yawl rigged fishing boat had paid off, and I was granted my first mate's ticket.

My first trip on board *Falmouth Packet* was for a weekend visit to St Peter Port, Guernsey, with twelve teenage members, the full-time skipper, myself as first mate, and a young bosun. It was my opportunity to familiarise myself with the boat, to get the feel of sailing a large ketch, to have twelve willing hands to organise with the sailing, and to do all the chores which are necessary to keep the boat running smoothly.

Of course I was expected to climb the very tall mast, which I found to be a very daunting task the first time I did it. However, I soon became blasé about it, and by the time we returned to Plymouth I was full of admiration for the OYC and I had gained enough confidence to take on the responsibility of being a first mate.

A Delivery Run from Plymouth to the Hamble

The end-of-the-season trip was to deliver the *Packet* to Hamble for a winter refit. The crew consisted of the permanent skipper, myself as first mate, second mate, and an assortment of interesting adult club members.

A two-day stop-over was planned at Salcombe, so I asked the skipper if we could rig the dinghy, so that we could have some fun sailing it. He agreed and said that it would be easier than rowing the crew ashore. The last evening the second mate and I enjoyed a drink or two at the Island Cruising Club. The time came to return to the boat, taking with us the last two crew members. One was a young lady of slight build, and the other young lady was large and heavily built.

The second mate suggested that it would be a good exercise to see how well they could row us back to the boat. He sat in the bows keeping a look-out for obstacles, like quaysides, boats, buoys and river banks. Unfortunately the larger rower was about four times more powerful than her friend, so we proceeded in a series of circular motions, until we finally arrived at the boat, the sound of laughter still echoing around the moorings.

Next morning a bleary-eyed crew reluctantly braced themselves for a boisterous passage through the Start Point race. Nobody wanted to cook or make tea, so it fell to me to do that.

The boat was so far heeled to port that I had to tie the kettle down, with the spout pointing to starboard to prevent the kettle emptying itself. I then opened six tins of Fray Bentos steak and kidney pie, and put them in the pre-heated oven, before preparing the vegetables. A quarter of an hour later the boat changed tack without any warning. Oh no!!! The oven door flew open, and the pies scattered across the cabin, leaving it decorated with cow pats. Nobody was up to eating the remnants of the pies, as they did not mix well with seasickness and hangovers.

I was given command for the crossing of Lyme Bay, with instructions that the skipper would change over near Portland Bill. It was a fast crossing which I enjoyed immensely. I even climbed the main mast to take a photo of *Packet* heeled over, and making ten knots.

I told the Skipper that we would have to change course as we were getting close to Portland Bill. 'Nonsense,' he replied and produced a station-keeper to check our distance off. 'How do you know we are so close?' I pointed to my sextant, and said that I had already preset the angle of elevation of the lighthouse, as a safety measure.

Springing to attention he took command, and we rounded Portland Bill into Weymouth Bay, where the wind velocity increased considerably. *Packet* was now flying along at a breakneck pace, and we stormed through a flotilla of naval vessels which were leaving Portland Harbour.

The crew did a magnificent job in dropping all the sails, and bagging them in record time. We continued under way at a remark-

35

able speed to a mooring near the bridge, but had to use the engine as a brake.

Once ashore, the second mate and I headed for the Royal Dorset Sailing Club, where we found its facilities dated back to Victorian times. We asked the steward if we could take a shower, but we were advised to adjourn to the bar, as there were baths only, and it would take at least a half an hour for the boiler to provide enough water for one.

The solitary member in the bar asked us which boat we had in such an offhand manner that implied he owned a superior yacht, and judging by our lack of blazers, we no doubt had arrived in a bathtub. I said that ours was the *Falmouth Packet*, which he had witnessed making a spectacular entrance. He thawed out and admitted that he owned a very small bilge keeler. By then our bathwater was ready and I appreciated the novel experience of using an early Victorian bath.

Next day we all enjoyed the delights of sailing whilst watching the Dorset and Hampshire coast unfold, as we headed for our last stop-over in the Cowes marina. I was very impressed with close up views of the Needles, and enjoyed sailing in waters where I had raced a catamaran some forty years ago.

We moored up alongside a French customs cutter which had just escorted a cross-Channel race. The captain seemed interested in *Packet* and her crew, so I decided to chat him up in French. The outcome was a suggestion that we held a combined party on board our boat.

This turned out to be the best evening's entertainment we could have hoped for. One of our crew was a brilliant guitarist, and another a very good raconteur. Each member of the French customs boat came from a different region of France, and they all took turns to sing their regional song. At one stage the singing stopped suddenly, and all eyes turned to see a ghostlike figure appear in the gloom of the cabin. To our horror it was a middle-aged male member of our crew, dressed in a diaphanous negligee! Our skipper quickly banished him from the cabin, never to be seen again.

Figure 9   Rough water.

The next morning I was surprised to see the French captain with a bottle of pastis in one hand and a glass in the other, teaching his first officer how to play hopscotch on the pontoon. He assured me that the *Falmouth Packet* and its crew would have the freedom of Cherbourg's harbour, and a standing invitation to one of their parties whenever we visited his harbour.

Our skipper rose to the occasion; he ordered us to hoist sail and make our way up the river, then turn and sail past the cutter, whilst he played a recording of us all singing, backed by our crew, who lined the rail and sang in unison as loudly as possible.

Reluctantly we left for the Hamble, where *Falmouth Packet* remained for her winter refit.

7

An Offer I Could Not Refuse

One of my favourite spots in Looe was Curtis and Pape's boatyard. I often called in to buy some timber and other items I needed for my own projects, and for my senior pupils' projects. Alan Pape, the well-known designer, and the Yard manager, Mick Marshall, were always very helpful, and generous.

I was surprised when on one occasion Alan said he would like to have a chat in his office. This sounded rather ominous. However, he explained that there was a recession in the trade, and he was desperate to find work for two of his key staff. I had told him that I hoped one day I would have enough money to buy one of his boats. I knew that he had taken an interest in my sailing, but I was overwhelmed by the generous offer he made me.

He wished to try out a prototype half-tonner racing yacht, which could be scaled down to twenty-two feet overall. He offered to give me the design at no cost. His two best men would build the hull, plant the keel and install the rudder, complete the deck, bulkheads and coach roof and make and fit the stanchions and pulpit. Finally, they would fit a small second-hand two-stroke engine.

I was also to be given free use of the yard, so I could finish it myself. All for the ridiculously cheap price of £2,000. How could I possibly refuse? An early decision was essential for the future of the yard. A colleague and friend lent me £1,000 the next day, without me even asking for it. My mother lent me the rest, so it was all systems go.

Naturally I hoped my family would enjoy my new toy and my ambition was to complete all the outstanding work in time for next season's sailing. I hoped the trials would please Alan Pape and the boat would be suitable for the OSTAR (Offshore Single-handed Transatlantic Race), because I fancied entering the next race if I measured up to the challenge. Sail training appealed to me as a means of financing the running of the boat.

My son Paul and I worked throughout the winter; at times it was so cold I thought we would become frozen to the job. Spring came early and we thawed out, and there was a beautifully varnished, four-berth yacht which I had once only dreamed of owning. I owed a great deal to Paul for all his hard work, and to Alan Pape and his team at the boatyard.

A small crowd gathered for the launching ceremony. I named my

Figure 10   Launch of *Espinet*.

pride and joy, after one of my ancestors called 'Espinet'. The let-down to the event was to find that the seacock had been left open, which left *Espinet* and me with a sinking feeling that my many seafaring ancestors would have had a laugh at my expense.

Espinet's Sea Trials

Espinet's sea trial led me to discover the joys of handling a fast and well balanced yacht, which could turn on a sixpence with only the mainsail set. So far I could find no fault whatsoever. It remained for me to sail in big seas and very strong winds, and over a substantial distance, before I would know if she was seaworthy enough for an Atlantic crossing. A visit to the Isles of Scilly should be far enough to test her for the time being. Paul, Joe Stephenson (a very good friend of mine) and I set off with high expectations, and a Force 6 northerly wind to help us on our way.

At one stage we maintained a minimum speed of ten knots for one and half hours. This was partly due to her timbers being still dry, and we carried very little excess weight. It was a very fast passage, but I regretted that I hadn't kept a log.

Hugh Town harbour was chock-a-block with visiting boats, and it was just like trying to find a space in Tesco's car park when everyone is doing their weekend shopping. We squeezed into a space fairly close to the Lifeboat ramp, then pumped up the dinghy and set off in search of a decent meal. We settled for the cafeteria on the harbour, where the Prime Minister and his very personal secretary were having their lunch in a quiet corner.

After lunch we opted for a 'busman's holiday', by having a boat trip to Tresco. A long walk round the tropical gardens induced a craving for a long cool beer at the island's pub, which was renowned for its all-night drinking hours. The landlord had assumed that he was never going to be raided, because it was too dangerous to sail at night, amongst the islands and rocks. One memorable night, however, the Cornish Constabulary descended upon the crowd of beer-sodden late-nighters and their host. What a pity!

The balmy night air, and the final cup of tea, helped the three of us drop off into a deep sleep. Hours later, loud banging noises, a clanking of heavy metal, a loud explosion, followed by the whoosh of the lifeboat as it was launched, woke us up with a jolt. The early news from the waterfront was as bad as it gets. Leaking gas and a lit cigarette caused the explosion and fire destroyed a yacht anchored at Tresco. The husband who was near the hatchway escaped, but his wife burned to death in the pyre which had once been their yacht. It was almost possible to feel and touch the sadness that settled on the island.

Before leaving, we sailed round the Bishop Rock Lighthouse, which is the tallest in the United Kingdom and dominates the Isles of Scilly. Little did I realise that one day I would sail past it after sailing back from Ireland in a very severe storm.

We continued sailing until we reached our planned stopover at Newlyn harbour, arriving after dark. I was advised to anchor away from the noise and disturbance of the fishing fleet, close to the road. The tide dropped and left *Espinet* grounded. I quickly fixed the starboard leg, but was unable to fit the other because something was in its way. The only way to avoid the boat falling over onto the obstacle was to keep the maximum weight possible on the starboard edge. It was far too dangerous to move about, so the three of us spent two hours in our pyjamas, sitting with our legs over the side and being surrounded by the heaviest things we could find. Gaggles of giggling women passed by, on their way to the seven o'clock shift. Their ribald comments, and their gesticulations, reduced the ego of the proud owner of his new yacht to rock bottom. However, we managed to make it back to Looe without any further mishaps.

Figure 11 *Espinet* moored at Looe circa 1994.

Raincoat, Trilby and Black Shoes

Shortly after my return from the Scillies my parents spent a holiday in Looe, so I invited my father, an ex-quartermaster, to come out sailing with me to Fowey. He was delighted with the chance to

42

be back on the water again, and said he would meet me on the quay.

I am ashamed to say that I was embarrassed to see Dad, kitted out in a raincoat, Trilby hat, black polished shoes and neatly creased trousers – was he dressed ready for church?

However, I thoroughly enjoyed every minute of our time together. It appeared to me that I was sailing with the young seaman who had run away to sea and not the elderly gent dressed for a church service at Bexhill-on-Sea. I shouldn't have been surprised that Dad helmed my little boat so well – after all, he had steered huge liners round Cape Horn, and sailed around the rest of the world.

I Change Course

I had been waiting for an opportunity to see how *Espinet* would make out in gale conditions. An opportunity soon arose for Joe, Paul and me to take a break. A whole week would be long enough to visit Roscoff and be back in time for school, providing the weather was settled enough.

The day of our departure, a Force 7 northerly was the strongest we could expect for the crossing. By the time we had passed the Eddystone Lighthouse it looked like being a rough crossing. I realised that with a fetch of over a hundred miles, the Breton coast would be a dangerous landfall. Some five miles beyond the lighthouse, a violent gust of wind knocked us down. Fortunately, we didn't take on any water, nor did the sails, so righting the boat was straightforward.

To continue would be stupid, so we changed course for Falmouth, hoping we would find some respite as we closed the land. Beating to windward in rough seas and into stronger winds was a very cold, wet and exhausting experience. The steward at the Royal Cornwall Yacht Club said they had been expecting us, because the lighthouse keepers had seen our knockdown, and had informed the coastguard and the club.

I was very relieved I had made the right decision, but this sea trial had shown that *Espinet* could be driven into rough seas and strong winds, providing she kept enough canvas up. The weather system moved away, leaving us to enjoy sunshine and a leisurely return home.

8

The Looe Sailing School

My plans to start teaching sailing professionally began to take shape when I sold *Charlotte* and built her replacement. The next step was to apply for a Waterman's licence, for plying for hire while under sail. I was examined by two well-known 'J class' vintage sailors, Alfred John and Jack the harbourmaster. They were particularly interested in my last cruise in *Charlotte* and wanted to know lots of details, some of which I was embarrassed to relate.

They both laughed, and then recounted how on their first fishing trip the other side of the Channel, they went aground on the Minquees on a falling tide. They too lacked a dinghy and experience. The crew survived by repairing the damage while their boat sat precariously on the sharp rocks. Alfred John said, 'There are those who do go sailing and make mistakes, but if they survive and learn by their experiences they go on and become real sailors.' I was granted the very first Waterman's licence to ply for hire under sail from Looe in Cornwall.

The local town council authorised my application for me to establish the Looe Sailing School, which was licensed to operate between Plymouth and Fowey. Every year *Espinet* had to be inspected for seaworthiness. My enterprise was then registered with the Board of Trade.

Sailing Lessons

My first group of pupils were studying 'Sailing for Beginners' at evening class, which I had organised to cover theory, along with a

45

day cruise during the Easter break, when they took turns to navigate, helm, crew and make tea.

Casual trade introduced me to some very interesting characters, and they were all very enthusiastic. For my part, I felt that I was taking their money under false pretences, because I was enjoying myself so much. During the summer months I kept very busy teaching French students from the Vacances Studieuses Françaises organisation, in batches of four fifteen-year-old boys, for three-hour practical lessons on board *Espinet*. All the lads were very well behaved, and seemed to enjoy themselves as much as I did.

However on one trip things did not go according to plan. I had left *Espinet* anchored in Looe Bay because the tide was out, and I planned to ferry my crew two at a time to the boat, but when I arrived at the beach the wind was Force 7 and the sea was choppy inside the bay, so I decided to cancel the trip.

The four lads were very disappointed. They insisted that they could swim out to the boat if necessary, and they were not afraid of a little wind. They implied that I was afraid to venture out. Stupidly I fell into their trap, and I agreed that we could sail in the sheltered area, in the lee of Looe Island. The lads soon got fed up with pottering about inshore, and again suggested I might be chicken. Foolishly I changed my mind, and told them we would make for Fowey, but if the wind increased we would immediately return to Looe. The strongest sailor was at the helm whilst I watched and assessed the crew, weather and the sea state. Suddenly a 'white out' appeared through the mist. Two of the crew had just enough time to bundle the jib through the fore hatch as it struck! The helmsman was the only competent sailor, and was game to keep the helm. I crewed and instructed him as we battled our way from the lee shore, under mainsail only. The others remained below, scared out of their minds.

I kept a wide berth from Looe Island, and met up with some fishing boats hurrying back to the safety of the harbour. *Espinet* still under mainsail only, maintained eleven plus knots as she overtook the leading fishing boats. What a fine sight we must have made, with a bow wave sixty feet wide, as she tried to get up on 'the plane'.

As we approached the Banjo Pier cries of alarm and dismay came from below because I had to turn back to sea, as the tide was too low for us to enter the river. Waiting for over an hour must have seemed like an eternity for the three seasick lads who stayed below.

Next morning all four lads turned up to scrub out, and to offer their apologies. Much to my surprise they all wanted to sail with me again. Somewhere along the line we had all learned something worthwhile.

9

Ireland and Espinet*'s Last Sea Trial*

For several years I had set my sights on entering the single-handed Transatlantic race. With this in mind I needed to put *Espinet* and myself through one last trial, and sailing to the south-western coast of Ireland and returning via the Isles of Scilly seemed a pretty good test.

However, it was Paul, Joe and I who set off on 21 August 1973 for Ireland, with just over two weeks to complete the trip. Our first visitor was a Nimrod flying very low, which banked and did a 360-degree turn with us in the dead centre. I just hoped we wouldn't see another one searching for us in earnest. Our next visitor was the *Golden Hind*, which crossed ahead of us on its way to Falmouth. We spent our first night at anchor just North of Mullion Island, to unstick the compression rings in our second-hand two-stroke engine. We spent the second night comfortably moored up to the outer quay at Penzance harbour, so that we would have a good night's sleep before the long crossing to Crosshaven in County Cork.

The visibility was poor, and my navigation was by dead reckoning, so I needed a very accurate fix before we left the Longships Lighthouse. I preset the sextant to establish the safe distance off, and we sailed directly towards the lighthouse. Two of the keepers came down onto the rock to watch us, thinking we intended to land for some reason. But we waved to them and turned towards Ireland, with a northerly Force 2/3, swell and a sea mist to keep us company.

Joe and then Paul followed me in keeping two-hourly watches, starting at 1800 hours. By 1600 hours the next day the wind had become easterly Force 1/2.

Our next visitors were a family of porpoises who decided to play with *Espinet*, while chatting to one another all the time. Follow the leader started with the youngest and ended with Dad being 'tail end Charlie'. 'I can leap higher than you, I can swim closer to this boat than you can' ended with Dad banging himself against the keel. The family, still chatting, or rather squeaking away to one another, sped off ahead of us.

Shortly afterwards we saw hundreds of them migrating in family groups. Fish were leaping out of the water to avoid being eaten by the porpoises or by the flocks of sea birds dive-bombing them. We continued on our way, leaving the sounds and sights of frenzied feeding behind, but keeping memories with us, which are still as vivid today as they were all those years ago.

Eventually we sighted Kinsale Head Lighthouse 10 degrees to port, making my dead reckoning navigation rather suspect. After establishing a reliable fix, we continued on to White Bay where we anchored for a rest, refreshed and relieved that we had arrived at the correct island. We continued on to Crosshaven to an excellent reception at the sailing club, having covered 243 miles without mishap.

My enquiries about getting customs and excise clearance met with blank looks and evasive replies; people seemed to have their own reasons for not wishing to see the customs officers. Finally the steward telephoned to get our clearance. A tall, young, anorexic junior officer and his short, fat superior arrived at the pontoon and asked how they would get to our boat. Both were horrified at the prospect of being taken out to *Espinet* in our four-man rubber dinghy, because neither of them had ever been in one before. The youngster remained ashore while I paddled out to the boat, where the necessary forms were completed, as beads of sweat dripped onto them from the officer's face.

When he had finished he said, 'You will be locking your boat up when you go ashore, sir?' 'No,' I replied. 'To be sure you will be locking her up?' 'But there isn't a lock,' I said. 'Why is that?' he asked. Not wishing the poor soul to be offended, I said I thought the Irish were like the Cornish, and I hadn't any reason to lock the boat up before. 'Well to be sure the Irish are honest, except for the odd one, three, five, seven and nine that aren't.'

However, he warned me that if the wind continued turning to the west, there would be seas only seen in the southern oceans. Warning bells began to ring when other folk asked if we were staying for the winter, as it was nearly the end of the sailing season. They were very surprised when we told them we had to return home within a week or so.

Our need for a proper meal and some clean clothes seemed more pressing than the wind direction and our departure home, so off we went to Cork to find a restaurant and a laundrette. The meal was excellent, but the rest of the afternoon was spent looking for somewhere to wash our clothes. Everywhere we went with our bags of dirty washing, the Garda followed us in their car. I wondered if they suspected that we were English terrorists, trying to find the

Figure 12   Smallest yacht at Kinsale.

IRA's headquarters so we could blow it up. We returned to the boat, still with our dirty washing, to a 'powwow' to decide our plans for the rest of our stay in Ireland.

My original intention was to visit the south-western coast, so Kinsale was in the right direction, and not too far away if we needed to return home if there was any chance of bad weather showing up.

Kinsale turned out to be a quiet, pleasant spot where the locals seemed friendly, and it was an ideal spot to get our strength up for some more serious sailing. Once again, the locals were concerned about us having to make the crossing in our small boat, and with the risk of some very bad weather. I finally came to the conclusion that I was being given serious advice, and not being 'wound up', as is often the case.

That evening we walked to the local, and met a drunk weaving his erratic path towards us. He walked straight into a lamp post with a sickening thud, but continued on his merry way, smack bang into the next one. The Irish never do things by half!

What we needed was a reliable weather forecast for the rest of the week, before making plans for the rest of our stay. The following morning I telephoned the met officer at Shannon Airport, and asked him if he expected any bad weather for the rest of the week, as we would be sailing a small boat back to Cornwall. He said that within the next two days we could expect westerly Force 5–6 winds, with moderate seas and swell. If we missed this opportunity, it would be impossible to make the crossing this year, because a large and threatening weather system was heading our way from the other side of the Atlantic. We had no other option but to leave Kinsale in the morning.

Return to Cornwall, and the Final Sea Trial for *Espinet* and Her Crew

Our passage to the Isles of Scilly started at 0800 hours, with only a north-westerly breeze to fill the genoa and mainsail. Paul had the engine running to help us on our way for two hours. Once again we met up with a family of porpoises who were not in a playful mood as they were too busy looking for breakfast.

At 1200 hours on the skipper's watch, the wind was WSW Force 4 and the swell was pronounced. At 1400 hours on Joe's watch, the wind was WSW Force 4 with an increasing swell, and by 1600 hours on Paul's watch, the wind was Force 5 with moderate seas and increasing swell. At 2000 hours, with the skipper back on watch, the wind was Force 5 + with moderate sea and increasing swell.

Sail was reduced in anticipation of hardening of conditions and falling visibility due to limited light from the moon. I hoped that we would not have to do another sail change before first light.

At 0200 hours the next morning Paul was on the helm, with myself providing back up. A pitch black night, with the sound of breaking seas that sounded like express trains rushing past us. I could only imagine that the waves were bigger, the swell longer, and we were in the mire, well and truly!

Figure 13   Paul in charge of *Espinet*.

0600 hours, at first light and with poor visibility, and we were now in gale conditions, and when the peaks of the swell combined with huge waves, the results were spectacular, with very heavy foam streaks I could not believe we had been sailing in these conditions for some hours during the night

Now under storm headsail only, at speeds of 7-plus knots, *Espinet* took off from the top of a wave and fell through space, before hitting the water with a frightening bang. The same sequence, of flying and landing with a sickening bang, was repeated several more times. I wondered if our planted keel would fall off if we continued in the same way for much longer.

It became imperative to reduce our speed, but roller reefing the mainsail, until it was much smaller than the storm head sail, was the only option. Jeans and towels were rolled in so that they flattened the tiny sail area.

Even with the boat's speed down to 5 knots, *Espinet* succeeded twice more at flying in freefall before I discovered how to keep her in the water. On reaching the crest of the big waves, it was necessary to turn sharply so the keel acted as a brake. It was important to straighten up before losing the wind, about halfway into the trough, because it was necessary to build up speed to negotiate the next wave.

It was now a case of sailing for survival and avoiding the biggest of the freak waves, which I feared could capsize us. I decided to keep Paul down below, as I was afraid that he might well be put off sailing for life if he saw such frightening sights. I remained at the helm  for four hours, hoping that Joe would be fresh enough to cope with a two-hour stint.

In the meantime, strange things began to happen. A corona appeared briefly, which normally is not a good sign, then two columns of water, like giant rolls of linoleum, appeared behind us, one after the other some quarter of a mile away. Dense spindrift

Figure 14   Joe at the helm.

was soaking everything and making it difficult to breathe normally. Time had very little meaning, so I guess it was an hour later that we sailed on the very edge of a hole in the sea. The part I could see was the end of an elliptical hole, with sides steeper than I would believe, and the surface resembled the pattern of  falling water, which I had seen close up on the face of steep waves in a gale. I could not see the bottom of the hole, but I am certain that we would not have survived if we had fallen into it.

I decided not to tell the others about what I had seen, especially as we had passed another hole a couple of hundred yards away. I had managed to avoid some of the biggest waves, and felt more confident about sailing in dense spindrift.

54

Figure 15   The wall of death.

At 0900 hours we mounted the peak of the swell, and from this vantage point I could see a wall of water, about a quarter of a mile in length, rising in front of us, and it looked as though it would collapse towards us. This in my mind was impossible because, all the waves were breaking in the opposite direction. I decided to maintain the maximum speed possible, and to meet the 'wall' head on. The cabin hatch was closed all the time as a safety measure, but I had to keep hold of the tiller, and the only refuge I had would be to lie in the bottom of the cockpit.

Espinet was nearly falling over backwards, as her bows split the ten feet of solid white falling water. I was standing upright like a sentry in his box, when the daylight disappeared as the sea passed over us! Severely shaken by the experience, I asked Joe to take a two-hour watch, while I briefed him on how to cope with the 'big ones'. Joe coped very well during his watch, and when I took over again he said, 'Guess what I've seen? A hole in the sea!'

The first sign of human life was a large cargo vessel barely making way towards the Bristol Channel, and about this time the visibility began to improve. We then saw what I believe to be a Russian spy ship, keeping station. It was the only other vessel we saw during our entire journey from Ireland to Looe which had braved the storm. For a few brief minutes the visibility improved enough for us to

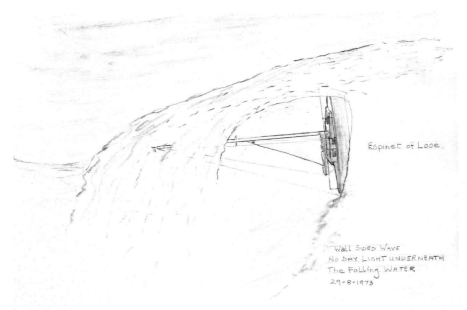

Figure 16   Wall-sided wave.

Figure 17   Spy ship hove-to on crest of swell.

spot some land, but there was no way I could identify it. We held our course as the mirage evaporated in the mist, and a lighthouse appeared in its place.

By this time my few remaining brain cells had failed to function,

Figure 18   Huge waves and massive swell.

through stress and overwork. We had made our planned landfall, and there was the Bishop Rock Lighthouse. However, I kept on thinking that we might be rounding the Longships Lighthouse instead. All three of us watched the awesome sight of the seas running up the tower for over two-thirds of its height. The rise and fall of the swell was equally awesome, as all the hidden rocks became exposed every few minutes. Perhaps we were sailing over some, without knowing.

As we rounded the lighthouse we began to find shelter in the lee of the islands. It was dark before we turned north into Crow Sound, where we found peace from the elements. My brain was still playing tricks on my logic, because I actually wondered if we had turned into Mounts Bay in Cornwall!

Our peace of mind was instantly shattered when we grounded on the bar, and the tide was going out. None of the usual tricks to get ourselves into deeper water worked, but Joe was game to row the dinghy, and drop the main anchor in deeper water, which was easier said than done. It worked, so we then winched and motored ourselves out of trouble, and stayed anchored, sleeping like logs.

The next morning we slept in until midday, expecting to stay in the harbour, but we found it closed and had to find another refuge, which turned out to be just the other side of the road. By anchoring in only six inches under the keel at low water, we avoided the waves which continued to batter the isles. Shore leave, as you can imagine after our ordeal, was pure bliss. Our first cooked meal for two days, a few pints, and walking on firm ground without having to hold onto something were to be savoured. Then we stocked up for the homeward run.

PUBLIC HEALTH (SHIPS) REGULATIONS 1970

CERTIFICATE OF FREE PRATIQUE

Port	*Scilly*	Date of arrival	*30.8.73*
Ship	*Espinet*	From	*Kinsale*

I have examined *R. Bishop* Master of the above ship and under the above Regulations
(Name)
I hereby grant the vessel free pratique.

Stamp of Issuing Authority
H.M. CUSTOMS & EXCISE CUSTOM HOUSE
ISLES OF SCILLY

_____ (Signature)

_____ (Signature) *Brown*

Authorised Officer of the Port Health Authority
or
Customs Officer

Time _____ Date *30-8-73*

C304 Gp3642 (147382) 908829. 500M. 12/71 S(P&D)L

Figure 19   Certificate of Free Pratique.

The Way Home from St Mary's

Having fully recovered from our ordeal, and having enjoyed our brief stay in Hugh Town, we set sail under jib and full mainsail for Penzance on the 31 August 1973. The gale cone was still hoisted, but we had the advantage of a following wind. Paul's eyes stood out like organ stops when we started to ride the big seas and long swell.

Joe and I were now full of confidence and thoroughly enjoyed sailing the ups and downs of Nature's great switchback. With twenty-mile visibility, the vistas from the tops of bigger waves were unforgettable. We arrived at Penzance all too quickly, and with my adrenaline still keeping me on a high.

On 4 September 1973, with cirrus and lower clouds present and gale cone still up, we set sail for St Mawes with a SW gale forecast. We avoided the Welloe this time and kept in the lee of the land, as we beat out via Loe Bar, Mullion isle and the Lizard. It was difficult to keep off Menhyr Rock, but we arrived as planned at St Mawes, having averaged 5.5 knots. So far, we had been the only ones at sea since leaving St Mary's.

At 0700 hours on 6 September we set sail for our final leg of the cruise, in light winds, racing several larger yachts which were heading in the same direction as us. The other skippers were none too pleased with our superior performance, as we maintained five knots in such light winds.

At 1255 hours on 6 September 1973 our holiday cruise of 606 nautical miles ended with one unexpected disappointment. The minimum OA (Over All) length of 22 feet had been increased to 24 feet, making *Espinet* ineligible for the next OSTAR. Our safe return was met with little enthusiasm by my wife, indicating that it was our marriage which was too close to the rocks, and not *Espinet*'s course.

Passage Kinsale to the Isles of Scilly: Post-mortem

I have always tried to underestimate conditions at sea, for fear of otherwise sounding like a fisherman and his elasticated arms, which stretch as he describes his latest catch. It is reassuring when there is independent evidence to compare what actually happened with my recollections, or what I recorded in my log.

At the height of the storm we were sailing, when a rescue operation was in progress to raise a mini-submarine which was stranded on the sea bed off southern Ireland, the TV and press reported that the rescue operation had been cancelled because the helicopters were unable to fly, as the waves were forty feet high, with storm-force winds, and the visibility was very poor. In addition, the swell was exceptionally long between crests.

In those days weather ships in the Atlantic provided the information which was used for forecasting, and not satellites which are used today. It transpired that an occluded front had not been noticed, so no warning was given. Prolonged easterlies were followed by strong westerlies which caused the exceptional swell, and the strong tides made matters worse. It is beyond my understanding why so many strange things happened during the crossing. The length of the swell astounded me, having witnessed a Force 11 southerly from some high cliffs near Looe. The swell was dramatic but much shorter than we encountered, because the fetch was only about one hundred miles, whereas the Atlantic fetch was over two thousand miles.

The most severe conditions lasted from 0500 hours to 1100 hours, and the tiny amount of reefed mainsail gave us an average of 6.7 knots. At this time the sea state took on the look of a Force 10. At one stage I was transfixed by the sight of the huge waves breaking, losing height but hurrying to catch us up, and threatening to engulf us. Each time the boiling water reached us it swept *Espinet* onto her port side and we were carried away sideways at five knots with the side deck awash.

The one moment of truth came when we tried to mount the 'wall of water' and almost did a backward somersault under water. I faced the stark truth that I had risked the lives of my son and my friend because I had wanted to take part in the OSTAR the following year.

Years later when the Fastnet race unfolded and I saw the conditions were no worse than we had experienced, I realised that the three of us did well to survive the storm in such a small boat, and coped better than some of the crews.

If the met officer had been able to warn me about the impending storm, I certainly would not have attempted the passage.

The Flying Espinet

Figure 20   *Espinet* falling off a breaking forty foot wave.

10

Morning Cloud

My last opportunity to sail before the end of the season coincided with my marriage ending up on the rocks, so I thought it would be good to have some time on my own cruising Plymouth's fine waters, to sort out some vexing problems. I have always enjoyed sailing on my own in strong winds, and inland the sudden gusts and changes of wind direction keep me on my toes. However, I had promised my son Paul that I would let him skipper *Espinet* back to Looe, with me as his crew.

By the time he arrived in Plymouth there was a strong southern swell and a Force 8 south-easterly wind. I considered that it was not prudent for me to keep my word. Teenagers can be very persistent at times. He said that he had sailed *Charlotte* in bad weather, so why not *Espinet*, which had survived the storm earlier? I knew that he was man enough for the job, so I agreed, but only on my conditions. The first condition was that he stayed at the helm until we had reached far enough offshore to make a good course towards Looe.

He would also have to sail with a full mainsail and the jib, in order to have enough power to drive us through the big seas. It was going to be a very wet and rough ride. Paul rose to the challenge, and he paid attention to my advice. He reached his target distance, tired out and soaked through and was not unduly put out by the breaking seas running up the jib.

I took over the helm and left Paul to crash out in the very wet cabin. My tack provided me with some superb sport, surfing down the face of the breaking waves, and hopping back up to the top of the next one. The routine continued until we were passing Rame Head. I was in my element!

Suddenly, an even larger wave caught me unawares, when it broke quicker than I expected, knocking me over the stern, but still clutching the rear end of the tiller for dear life. My fitness and strength saved my life, as I hauled myself back into the cockpit. Paul was asleep at the time, and may well have remained so, leaving *Espinet* to her own devices, if I had fallen overboard. She would most probably have turned towards the rocky headland before he had woken up.

All the time I had been surfing, I felt that a third person was sitting beside me, was enjoying the sport, and somehow had made me grip the tiller so tightly, which saved our lives.

I have often wondered if my other companion was the spirit of one of my many seafaring ancestors. I expect he would be saying, 'You silly b...! Next time remember to wear a life jacket and harness, and clip it on.'

On the TV news that evening, it was announced that Edward Heath's yacht, *Morning Cloud*, had broken up at sea, with the loss of its crew. This tragic loss illustrated the importance of sailing only sturdy craft, with experienced crew, in bad weather. Life jackets and harnesses are not just for decoration.

Clubs and Pubs

Espinet was due to be put in the boatyard for the winter in a few days' time, leaving Saturday free for sailing. However, the conditions were rough, and Joe and Paul were both keen to join me in a visit to the sailing club at Fowey for a drink. As usual, the Blazer Brigade were propped up at the bar, and we felt out of place, being windswept, salt-stained and untidy.

One of the committee members asked where we had moored, so I pointed to *Espinet*. With a very disapproving look, and a superior voice, which was loud enough to be noticed, he said, 'Rather small isn't she?' I replied, 'She is only twenty-two feet overall, but we three have sailed her recently to Ireland, then sailed back in a severe gale. How far have you sailed your own boat?' I knew full well that he most probably only ever set foot outside the harbour in good weather. Little did I realise that the return trip to Looe was going to be my last one in dear *Espinet*.

Our little incident reminded me of a story which the steward at the Royal Cornwall Yacht Club related, after 'the blazers' had left. One winter's evening he was very busy serving a crowded bar, while a family of four sat by the fire, quietly enjoying its warmth. Nobody approached them, or spoke a single word to the visitors. After the crowd had left, the steward found time to make them feel at home.

It was obvious that the family had been sailing, by their weather-beaten faces and their worn jeans. Naturally he was curious to know where they had been sailing so late in the year. He was amazed to learn that they had sailed from New Zealand, and Falmouth was their first stop in the United Kingdom. He listened, enthralled by some of their experiences, which the club members could have enjoyed as well if only they had extended a hand of friendship to such a remarkable family.

I must say that in my own experience I prefer to visit the local waterside pubs, where the interesting characters and seafaring folk hang out. My friends and I have spent many a memorable evening in great company in pubs like the Ship at Polruan, just opposite the Fowey Sailing Club. My last session there ended with my girlfriend standing on the quayside demanding a taxi to take her back to Espinet 2, which was anchored in the river. I am happy to say that she sobered up, and has remained beside me for over thirty years through the ups and downs of our sailing, and our event-packed lives.

11

The Falmouth Packet: *A Visit to St Peter Port*

Mel, one of the Ocean Youth Club's voluntary skippers, asked me if I was free for a weekend trip on the *Falmouth Packet* as his first mate, and with a more mature man who had only the experience of sailing his own small boat, who was to be the second mate.

We were going to take a group of youngsters sailing for the weekend, and Mel was very keen to visit St Peter Port, in spite of a poor forecast for a night crossing. He said that *Packet* was a very sturdy sea-going ketch, which would cope with the expected Force 7 westerly wind.

Mel had plenty of experience of sailing the boat, so the second mate and I agreed to make the crossing. Mel sorted out the watch system, set the course, and then said he would be getting his head down until we sighted the two Guernsey lights. I was to take over command until then, and I was to keep an eye on the other watch, to ensure that everything went smoothly.

During the second mate's watch, the wind increased and the sea became rougher. He was not a happy bunny, and I realised that we were in for a very rough crossing if things got any worse. The boat was heeled over and began to ship water on the side deck. I woke Mel, who took a look at the conditions and the state of the boat. 'She will take a lot more than this, so carry on,' was his reply.

Soon after, the thunder and lightning started, and the noise of the breaking waves grew louder and louder! A few hours later I briefly saw the looms of the two lights, although I was not able to recognise their signals because of the poor visibility. Unfortunately these

Figure 21   The Ocean Youth Club's *Falmouth Packet*, 72-foot ketch.

lights appeared much further to the east than they should have done. Within a few minutes the two looms disappeared completely in the mist. This was a serious matter because I estimated that we would miss the Isle of Guernsey if we maintained the same course.

I immediately woke Mel, who could not believe we were so far off course. I insisted on what I had seen, and said that I had checked the angle the lights had made to our course. He altered course to compensate for the error. The lightning was showing us the sea state was much worse, and that we were grossly over-canvased.

At first light our situation was all too obvious. We were now running before a full gale, and in poor visibility. We desperately needed to drop the mainsail and swap the headsail for a smaller one before our situation became dangerous. Mel had already taken command, and detailed me to drop the mainsail with the help of the strongest crew. With the extra muscle power we could not pull the sail down its track.

It was a new sail, and it just happened it was the first time it had been used during the gale. Sod's Law was going to rear its ugly head at the worst possible moment. My team set about the task by sheeting in the boom as tightly as possible, and I then began pulling in the leech, with a bowline on the end of a mooring line. Each time the sail flapped I inched my way forward and the lads wound the rope round the boom.

I was using my body to take up some of the slack, when suddenly the mainsheet was released, and for a while I found myself clinging to the boom for my dear life, as I looked down into the raging sea.

Our combined efforts managed to reduce the sail to an untidy bundle, and it made the boat more manageable.

However, we still had to change the foresail to a smaller one. This was easier said than done, and in the process the sheet was too diffi-cult to control, and the flapping sail tore the stainless-steel fitting out of the sail. At last, however, the sail change was completed and the boat was under control.

The electrical storm continued to blank out the directional finder, and it was causing problems with the steering compass. I remem-bered the last time this had occurred when I was sailing *Charlotte* in Mounts Bay, when the compass reversed itself completely. We made a landfall in very poor visibility, not knowing where we had been for several hours.

When we did sight land it was not possible to be certain where we were. Paul, my son, had been one of the crew. He had been off duty and had been sleeping. With a fresh mind and some knowledge of the Channel Islands, he recognised the coastline we were following as the north coast of Guernsey.

Mel soon confirmed Paul's sighting, and he got us into St Peter Port under engine, much to everybody's relief. No sooner had we moored up securely than I was sent aloft, together with the strongest and most agile lad, to sort out the mess of ropes and the huge bundle of the mainsail.

Neither of us enjoyed our task of unravelling the ropes, and easing the sail runners down the track, and we both had an overwhelming desire for a hot coffee and some dry clothes. We all felt less embarrassed at the untidy state we had arrived in, however, and we were soon free to enjoy the rest of the day recovering from our ordeal.

Our Return to Plymouth

Throughout the day the gale conditions improved slowly, but we found it very hard going beating our way up the Little Russel, and crossing the very strong tidal currents which seemed to carry us away in the wrong direction. Mel gave me the job of navigating at this stage. This was difficult because of the frequent tacking in rough seas and in very poor visibility. By the time we had reached Plymouth Sound, the wind was still Force 7, and the sea was rough.

Once inside the breakwater we dropped sail, and Mel told me to take *Packet* into Millbay dock without using the engine. I was quite happy to use the windage and the flood tide, but I declined to enter the dock without using a sail or the engine. Mel relented, and started the engine. We were all very glad to be going back to our home comforts.

In retrospect I was satisfied that we had coped with all our problems, which had been caused by the electrical storm, using a new sail without checking it beforehand, and making the crossing in the first place. I have been caught out myself on many occasions by being too optimistic about a doubtful weather forecast. In this instance, the safest option would have been to alter course and make for the shelter in the lee of the Devon coast, when the two mates advised the skipper about the bad conditions.

Every crew member gained very valuable experience. Paul had been impressed by his trips with the OYC, and somewhere along the line he gained the ambition to become one of the club's full-time skippers. I was naturally very proud when he achieved this dream.

12

Winter Fishing Netted Two Fishermen

John, a friend of mine, owned a large fishing boat, which he used as an escape from the trials and tribulations of his profession. Occasionally I gave him a hand during the winter, helping him with his fishing. In return I had some of the fresh shellfish, and enough fish to feed my hungry tribe.

On a very cold and wintry day, he persuaded me to help him land his catch from his tangle nets, when the wind was against a spring tide. This was considered to be very dangerous. However, the nets had been left out far too long because of the bad weather. There was every chance that he would lose not only the catch, but the nets as well. I decided to repay a favour I owed John, and I just hoped we would not run into any trouble.

In a bitterly cold wind of Force 5–6 and rough seas, we set off to find the nets some five miles offshore. When we arrived at the marker buoy, John lay-to with the main engine ticking over to stem the tide. A strong gust of wind suddenly caused the boat to veer towards the buoy, and its rope wound itself round the revolving propeller. 'Sod's Law' had been invoked.

Sure enough we could not reach the buoy or its rope. It was vital that we did reach it, then wrap the net and rope round the side opposite the wing engine's propeller. This would leave us with an engine to get us back to the mooring on the river Fowey.

In desperation I took the boat hook, and John held my legs while I leant over the transom and fished around for the elusive rope. John managed to pull me, the boat hook and the rope on board. I was still shaking with exhaustion, cold, and fear when we began to secure the ruined gear, and cut us free.

By the time we reached Fowey and began heading upstream, the night was blacker than the ace of spades. I was obliged to sit on the foredeck, still shaking with the cold, and using a torch to pick out our way through the minefield of obstacles, while John responded to my hand signals from the warmth of the cabin.

Suddenly a bright light passed across the sky in front of us. It was the masthead light of a large clay boat, which was about to make a sharp turn round a bend in the river. We were about to ram it mid-ships!! It was impossible to turn left to avoid the ship, because the wing engine would only let us make a sharp turn to the right.

John had the presence of mind to open the throttle and spin us in a circle to the right, and we just missed the ship by a gnat's whisker, as it turned round the bend.

We continued up stream, where we attempted to find our way through the trots to the mooring. It was a hit-or-miss business because the boat had a mind of its own, and stubbornly insisted on turning right. Eventually John managed to get the better of his wayward boat, and we picked up the elusive buoy.

I was fortunate to survive; 'the accident waiting to happen', and, of course, the frostbite.

A Sense of Humour is a Fine Thing

The very first boating trip which I organised was for several members of staff and a group of sixteen-year-old pupils from my comprehensive school. I had hired a fishing boat with its skipper, who was the son of my boat-builder friend and an ex-pupil of the school.

I knew that Paul had a good sense of humour, and that he would be popular with his trippers. Our destination was a tiny harbour in St Austell Bay called Polkerris, where we planned to enjoy our picnic lunch and a drink in the pub for the staff. The trip down was spent in glorious sunshine together with a lot of good-natured banter. When we arrived, we unfortunately had to anchor in the bay because it was very low water, and without a dinghy we were unable to reach dry land. I managed to hitch a lift in a passing rowing boat, crewed by non-English-speaking sailors, who fortunately understood my sign language. I then hired a dinghy for the afternoon, and rowed everyone ashore.

There remained one last problem which was going to spoil my well-laid plans. However we all enjoyed our visit to this charming and unspoilt sea-side hamlet, and it was not until we were about to leave that I had to resolve the problem of returning the dinghy.

'You are the organiser, Dick, so you will have to return the dinghy and then swim back!' was Paul's solution. I returned the dinghy wearing my swimming trunks, then I turned my attention to the fishing boat, which was further away than I remembered.

Being a strong swimmer, the extra distance didn't worry me, so I plunged in and started swimming quite fast towards the boat. I began to imagine that I was not getting nearer, so I tried to swim faster, but without any effect. Paul, the rotten devil, was reversing with the engine ticking over, so that I would not hear it running.

Once the onlookers, especially the pupils, realised that I had realised that the engine was running, they started to laugh at me. I dived and swam towards the front of the boat, where I held on to the stem iron. I was now out of sight, so Paul reversed and turned, but I was still out of sight, and enjoying a free tow. I could hear that the laughter had stopped, and panic began to set in at my disappearance. The boat stopped, so I popped out of the water, to the relief of those on board.

Having turned the tables on Paul the practical joker, I went below to dry myself and get dressed. To my surprise the fore hatch opened, and Paul skilfully tossed an entire bucketful of water up in the air. It landed on my head, to the delight of the pupils.

Everybody agreed that they had been pleased with the trip, and the amusements, even though most of them were at my expense.

13

The Falmouth Packet *and the Bay of Biscay*

The stress of my marriage unravelling caused my thyroid to be over-active. I was referred to a specialist, who recommended that I had a two-week break from work and started a course of medication.

Some days later one of the OYC's voluntary skippers arranged an end-of-year activity for a group of sixteen-year old boys and girls, to learn how to sail the *Falmouth Packet*. They then were promised a visit to Brittany and the Bay of Biscay. However, there was a problem with finding another skipper or first mate to join the crew, because the only other adult would be the French teacher, who lacked any experience of sailing.

My own doctor thought that it would be an excellent idea for me to go sailing, and I would co-skipper. We all met at Millbay dock in Plymouth for the usual familiarisation of the boat, its gear, safety, household routine, etc. The two of us then selected our teams, which would be keeping four-hourly watches during the following six days.

We left the dock and made our way to Fowey, with constant changes of sails, tacking, helming, keeping look out, and so on. By the time we reached our anchorage at Fowey, it was easy to select the most competent member in my watch to be my team leader. He proved to be very reliable, capable and experienced for a sixteen-year old.

The following day we had a very hard slog to windward, in a choppy sea, and in poor visibility due to the constant rain. It did not take long for the young ladies to have a 'bad hair day'. Most of

Figure 22   Plymouth to Brittany at full speed.

the crew looked pallid, and some were seasick. We finally reached our destination at Falmouth, where the parents came onboard to see how their 'little dears' were being treated. I began to wonder if the parents would be confident that these bedraggled-looking youngsters would survive their adventure. For my part, I had already found enough potential to see us through the long passage to L'Abervrach.

The next morning we set sail to Brittany, and we settled into the rhythm of the port and starboard watches. The other skipper was obviously in charge of his pupils, but he asked me to observe the crew, who had come from a very wide variety of backgrounds, and give him a candid report on them at the end of the cruise. He then went on to explain that as both he and the French teacher had a pupil–teacher relationship with the crew, some difficult situations might arise for them, and I was to take on the roll of a tough disciplinarian when necessary.

Figure 23   A motley crew.

We all know how enthusiastic teenagers are to help with house-hold chores, and how they will avoid the washing up at all costs. On board, the rotas for these chores are enforced by the other members of the team, who are far more efficient in getting even the cleaning of the heads done.

The long Channel crossing passed without mishap, the pallid faces began to colour, and everyone was anxious to show that their watch was the best. The experienced sailors spent time in the chart room asking awkward questions about our navigation, as if they were worried that we had gone the wrong side of Ushant, and were heading towards the USA.

However, we did make an accurate landfall, and the passage into the anchorage was quite exciting, with a big swell and some real waves, to give our novices some experience of real sailing, and more interesting navigation for those who had shown an interest in the chart room on the way over. They were fulfilling their potential which I had noticed earlier.

Early next morning we set off westwards, bound for Camaret, which is on the further side of the Rade de Brest. On route we had to pass through the Channel du Four, which is narrow in one section, and has very strong tidal currents. Spirits were high, and the passage was undertaken in a very seaman-like manner. The sails were bagged, the mainsail covered and the anchor dropped in style. I was proud of our young crew, and shore leave was granted on the understanding that they behaved well, and did not drink the cheap wine.

We three adults chose a seafood restaurant for our celebratory meal for the successful Channel crossing. Halfway through our meal, our high spirits were dashed to the ground when one of the team leaders arrived to give us some bad news.

One of the lads had ignored the instructions about drinking the cheap plonk, and had consumed a large quantity of it. He had gone berserk, and was threatening to have his wicked way with the girls! The three of us abandoned our meal and returned to the boat as fast as possible, fearing the worst!

The lad needed to be restrained, and I feared that he was going to suffer from alcoholic poisoning. It would be difficult to get a doctor quickly enough, before the damage was done. I suggested that we should pump him out by laying him face down over the edge of the boat, and pressing his back firmly. Thank goodness we managed to get rid of a large quantity of the red wine, which dyed the side of the boat, and it was very difficult to get rid of the evidence. For at least another hour the lad had to be restrained, because we feared he would have an accident if he was left to his own devices. We then took it in turns to walk our drunk round the deck, and plied him with black coffee until it was safe to put him to bed.

To make matters worse, the skipper went down with food poisoning, caused by some bad seafood which he ate the night before. He was in no condition to even appear on deck, let alone take charge of his own watch. The forecast was as bad as the skipper's stomach. Our time was running out for us to meet the deadline to be back in Plymouth. This meant I would have to take charge of both watches, and make the passage through the Channel du Four in near gale-force conditions, against a foul tide and a very strong wind, to reach L'Abervrach.

The skipper, woken by the rough motion of the boat, appeared looking grey-faced and concerned at what he saw. *Packet* was making a spectacular job of forcing her way through the narrow section of the dreaded Channel du Four, against the strong adverse current and into a gale-force 8 wind. The Skipper took command and started the engine in case it was needed. I was told to drop the head sail, because we were now over-canvased.

I chose the strongest and most dependable lad to help me. I clipped his harness on to the pulpit and instructed him to bundle the sail when I released the halyard, and drop it down the hatch. One of the 'difficult' lads had decided to sit by the main mast, and was preventing me from releasing the halyard. The boat was now crashing through large waves, sending the dense spray high above the lad who remained harnessed to the pulpit. The truculent lad was jeopardising the boat and our lives. He refused to move. Picking him up by his oilskins, I said, 'If you don't get below, I will throw you down there.' A kick up the backside persuaded him to change his mind.

My role as a hard man saved the day, and we were able to drop the head sail and get the boat under control, but it was the lad on the pulpit who deserved our thanks for staying put in frightening circumstances.

Our crisis was soon over, and it gave me quite a buzz seeing the youngsters enjoying the thrill of real sailing. Whilst we were tucked up safely in L'Abervrach for the night, the conditions improved considerably. The next morning I was greeted by sunshine, calmer sea, and the crew in high spirits at the prospect of telling their parents about their adventures.

On the way home, in mid-channel, the dinghy was lowered so that one of the lads and I could take some photos of *Packet* under way. The rotten b. .s sailed away towards the horizon, without leaving us with a dry crust of bread or a single drop of water. The crew,

Figure 24   Sixty miles to the nearest land.

however, decided that they could not manage without the dinghy, so they returned to pick us up. Nevertheless they enjoyed their prank.

A while later when I was sitting below near the companion way, I heard the lad who had refused to move away from the mast telling his friend how marvellous the cruise had been, and how he would like it to go on for ever. High praise from a lad from such a poor background, and with a bad police record.

Back at Millbay dock a group of boys who fancied their chances decided to tip me overboard, to settle some scores for bossing them about. I could see it coming, so I grabbed the nearest lad and tipped him over the rail, holding him by his feet. 'Right,' I said and pointed at the lad in front of me. 'Anyone moves and you will be next.' The remainder backed off as I hoisted my catch back on board. I was delighted to be told that the entire crew would like me to join them the following year for another cruise on the *Packet*.

This one event convinced me that the Ocean Youth Club's approach to sail training can have life-changing benefits, even for the most deprived and difficult youngsters.

A Curious Reaction to Rescue

Back in the days when my wife and I were still talking to one another, we invited another couple to an afternoon get together at our home, which had a superb view encompassing twenty-eight miles of the Cornish and Devon coast, as far as Bolt Head near Salcombe, and out to sea beyond the Eddystone Lighthouse. The curvature of the horizon was clearly visible that day.

Needless to say, our guests spent their time glued to the windows, fascinated by our view. The time came for afternoon tea and snacks, but Peter could not help glancing out to sea in between sandwiches.

Much to our surprise, he suddenly said, 'I think I have just seen some flares go up.' I followed the direction he indicated, and sure enough another flare was let off. I immediately called the coast-guard, who asked me to give the location and the type of vessel. A few minutes later the controller said that he was sending three fishing boats from Looe, as the Fowey lifeboat would take much longer to give assistance.

These three boats would fan out as they approached the small fishing boat, and I was asked to stay on the phone and say which boat was heading directly towards the distressed boat. It turned out to be the middle boat which was heading towards an eighteen-foot open fishing boat which was caught in a fishing net. When the skipper had been unable to cut the boat free, his clients began to panic.

The rescue had been very well controlled by the coastguard service, the fishermen had reacted without delay, and Peter's sharp eyes had saved the day by spotting the flares.

The following day, Specks and I took one another for a walk down to the East Looe Quay to check that my old boat was still floating after some very heavy rain, causing it to need to be pumped out. The father of the young skipper who had been rescued came striding towards me, clearly in a bad temper.

I hesitate to repeat exactly what he said, but it was not to thank me for calling out the coastguard. Instead, in good old Saxon language, he told me that I had no right whatever to call out the coastguard. The reason he was in such a foul temper was that he had lost face because his son had to be rescued. I could not believe that a fisherman could not be thankful that his son had been rescued.

14

Moving On and Espinet 2

My marriage finally sank in 1973, when we decided to divorce. It was a very stressful period in which my health, the well-being of my four children, and my finances suffered considerably. Being an optimist at heart, I hoped that one day I would find the perfect female, who would be good looking, intelligent, a good cook, sexy, and have the potential to become a good sailor.

It was unlikely that I could find the impossible, so I bought my dream boat, *Musketeer*, with my divorce settlement. Like my last boat, I named it after one of my French ancestors. *Espinet 2* was a twenty-eight-foot American cruising racing yacht which had been designed by Alan Pape, a well-known yacht and boat designer, and built with loving care by M. Marshall, the yard manager. I had fallen on my feet by finding a very fast boat with excellent sea-going qualities, *Musketeer* was a boat I had admired for several years.

It seemed like an eternity before my divorce settlement materialised. The Saturday before I took delivery, there was a knock on the door of my rented cottage. I opened the door and a very attractive blonde actually fell through the doorway, expecting to find the owner of the cottage at home.

That meeting was the beginning of our lives which have been joined at the hip ever since. My Mary has enriched my life beyond my wildest dreams, has tolerated my love of the sea, and has remained my first mate for over thirty years.

Prior to my meeting with Mary, I had been on the look-out for three crew members to join me on a long summer cruise visiting the Channel Islands, Brittany, the Bay of Biscay, and finally returning to Cornwall single-handed. Naturally I thought it would be an excellent idea to invite Mary to join Joe and me for my very first trip on *Espinet 2*. Much to my delight, she agreed to find out what sailing was really like.

When the day arrived for our trip, the sea was rough, and the wind was Force 7 offshore. I had a large spinnaker to play with, and I was determined to use it. I thought that if Mary could stand the ordeal which I had in mind for her, she would have the makings of a good sailor, and would be a perfect member of the crew for the planned cruise.

Grossly over-canvased with the spinnaker flying, and with the full mainsail set and the jib, we thrashed our way through the waves, with our stern wave desperately trying to poop us. I was carried away with the thrill of our ride, which lasted for fourteen miles out to sea in the English Channel. Suddenly the spinnaker halyard snapped!

Fortunately we recovered the sail without damaging it. The long and wet haul to windward and back to Looe gave me time to appreciate the comfortable way we rode the waves, and the handling qualities. By the time we reached the calmer seas near the land, I felt confident that *Espinet 2*, and Mary, could cope with the really bad conditions which we might encounter on a long cruise.

My most pressing problem was to find a way to persuade Mary to join me for the cruise. My run of bad luck which had haunted me for over two years evaporated when Mary agreed to crew for me. I was one happy bunny!

In the meantime, I was planning to squeeze in a weekend trip to the Channel Islands.

A Mini-Cruise for School Leavers

With the approval of the headmaster and the Education Department. I set sail in *Espinet 2*, for a three-day trip to St Peter Port on the isle of Guernsey, with three school leavers as crew. My son was

Figure 25   A French gaff-rigged cutter with top sail, used for sail training. Seen here off the Breton coast.

first mate and two sixteen-year-old girls were chosen by the staff for sail-training experience.

21 June 1975: 2100 hours. We cleared customs at Millbay dock in Plymouth. The forecast was SE Force 2 increasing later, visibility good. The girls worked well, and I was happy with the way Paul skippered when left in charge. We made an average of 5-plus knots for the 72-mile passage. It had been a very pleasant crossing and I hoped the crew had enjoyed the passage.

22 June 1975: 1600 hours. We entered the dock, which is right in the middle of town, and the crew were itching to be let off the leash. 'Behave yourselves, keep together, remember where the boat is moored, and don't be late back,' was my advice.

Their shore leave was a reward for their excellent behaviour so far. However, they could not resist the temptation to stalk me for the best part of the evening, so they could tell their mates back at school what mischief I got up to. Eventually I managed to shake them off by going to an adult-only pub for the rest of my night out.

Sunday was spent doing our own thing, and I am sure the crew enjoyed themselves as much as I did, until it was time to prepare for the return home. We left the marina after a disturbed meal, because we were running late, and nobody wanted to leave.

23 June 1975: 1630 hours. Departure time had arrived and we set off up the Little Russel channel, where we met rough seas and large waves. One freak wave lifted us up high and then dropped us like a lifeboat leaving its launching ramp. This shook me out of my complacency, and I wondered if the girls might panic, if they thought they would spend the whole crossing in such bad conditions.

It was certainly hard going, heading into the wind, until we cleared the strong cross currents north of the island. The wind began to freshen, and by nightfall it was NE Force 4–5. This made it more of a challenge for the girls who helmed, while either Paul or I kept watch for shipping. By the end of the night it looked as though the novices had been sailing in the dark for years, and they were enjoying it.

The skipper cooked breakfast and the told them to sail *Espinet 2* back to Millbay dock themselves, with Paul in charge of navigation. Later on we caught up with a Trident yacht, and raced it back to Plymouth. The girls took it in turns to sunbathe, so that their mates would be very jealous of their sun tans, and having the Monday off school.

24 June 1975: 1450 hours. Cleared customs at Millbay Dock.

I have happy memories of our trip to Guernsey, spent in the company of three sixteen-year-old pupils, or rather, as they became, three young friends.

15

Espinet 2: *Summer Cruise, July 1975*

Mary had agreed to come sailing with me, but she felt that she would like the company of another female, so we asked her American friend to join us as she had some experience of sailing. I agreed to take her as far as Guernsey, providing she contributed towards the cost of food and harbour dues, etc. A few days before we planned to set sail, she explained that she had a paying guest staying with her for the summer who was very anxious to join us, and he was willing to pay into the boat's kitty.

Mary had enough holiday time to continue with me as far as Roscoff, where she planned to return to Plymouth by the Brittany ferry. I would continue cruising on my own to the Bay of Biscay, and would then return to Looe single-handed, which would fulfil an ambition I had nurtured for some years.

19 July 1975: We cleared customs by midday, having qualified for duty free. I only just managed to squeeze it all into the chain locker, which I was instructed to keep locked until we left UK waters. At £1 for a bottle of scotch and 75p for a bottle of gin, I bought enough to last for several months. Once we had cleared the breakwater, I was relieved that we were under way, and very excited at the prospect of sailing to pastures new with Mary. With sunshine and a good wind, what more could I possibly ask for? To celebrate the start of our cruise, we raided the chain locker.

After a fine sail along the Devon coast, we arrived at Salcombe to find that it was so popular that all the moorings were taken, so we were obliged to spend the night in 'The Bag' (an anchorage outside the harbour), where we dragged anchor twice. We decided to forego

Figure 26   *Espinet 2*, East Looe Quay, summer cruise 1975.

the pleasures of Salcombe, and made an early start for our Channel crossing.

20 July 1975: Passage Salcombe to St Peter Port, Guernsey

Forecast: wind SW 4–5, moderate sea, visibility 2 miles.

We set sail under jib, staysail, and main, hoping to make our landfall before dark. It transpired that all the crew were novices, so they needed to master some basic skills very quickly, and keeping

85

lookout was one of the most important ones. Vessels on converging courses to our own would run into us, so it was vital to our safety for them to keep alert to this and other dangers, as there would be times when I would be below. With a rising wind and the visibility down to half a mile, the staysail was bagged. Cooking became nearly impossible to cope with in the rougher seas, and Mary became seasick, and suffered for the remainder of the crossing. Trusting the crew to keep a careful lookout, I decided to take a rest below so that I would be in good shape to cope with the navigation, strong currents and sailing in the dark. None of the crew had experienced deckwork in the dark or helming with only a compass as a guide, so I would have to be very vigilant, especially as there are very strong currents in the approach to the island.

I was enjoying my rest, and checked some details in the pilot guide and on the chart, as well as the tidal atlas. Everything was in order, or so it seemed, until I sensed that something was amiss. I popped my head out of the hatch, and was confronted by a very large bow wave bearing down on us with a large ship behind it. Unless I did something very quickly we would be rammed in a few minutes, and we were also on collision course with another ship. The crew were all chatting away, oblivious to our impending doom.

I grabbed the tiller and started playing Russian roulette, waiting for the big bang. We avoided the first ship but were caught by the bow wave which tossed us about, and within a few minutes we passed through the wash of the second vessel, so we were shaken and truly stirred. The whole incident seemed to last for an eternity, but in reality only went on for a few minutes. I can still recall the look of surprise, which changed to one of stark horror, when the crew thought they might drown. No doubt the whole incident was my own fault for expecting too much from novices.

1830 hours. The weather began to improve, but with lighter winds we were obliged to motor sail to overcome the strong foul tide. The welcome sight of Guernsey raised the crew's spirits, and we enjoyed a breathtaking sunset.

2230 hours. We entered St Peter Port marina, having averaged six knots for the crossing. It proved to be a very steep learning curve for the crew, but I had confidence that they would keep a good lookout in future.

A French yacht moored up alongside, and true to character, Mary made a hit with the skipper, who was anxious to get away from the continuous female chatter of his wife and sister-in-law. Mary and I soon made friends with our neighbours and thoroughly enjoyed their company. We also made the very best use of our time to tour the island and do the tourist things. Mary even found time to have a fabulous hair-do which cost her an arm and a leg, but was well worth every penny. Jean, our French friend, enquired about our plans for the rest of our cruise. I said that Mary and I were going to visit St Malo, Lezardrieux and Ile de Bréhat, and then go on to Roscoff where Mary would return to Plymouth on the Brittany ferry, because she would be starting work again. Our friends said that as we would be passing Perros-Guirec where they lived, they would be delighted if we would call on them.

In the meantime our two passengers pleaded with me to drop them off at Jersey, where they would take the ferry back to England. Mary and I agreed to their proposal. Our stay on Guernsey passed all too quickly, and we promised to call in to visit our friends on our way to Roscoff.

29 July 1975: Passage from St Peter Port to St Helier, Jersey

Forecast: SW 4–5 later 6. Good visibility, moderate to poor sea.

1015 hours: We left the marina with the tide setting us strongly towards the Isle of Sark. We all enjoyed riding the swell and some robust sailing until we met a ferry near Point Corbiere which was making hard going in the rough water. My crew looked very apprehensive when it dawned on them that they were sailing in the same rough seas and in a twenty-eight-foot boat.

1600 hours: We moored up to the island pontoon in St Helier harbour to our relief, and this time Mary was not sick, although

Figure 27 *Espinet 2*, St Helier, Jersey.

there was an unpleasant smell in the cabin. I resolved to give the boat a good clean up, and find out what was causing the smell. Mary and I made the most of our time together, although she was none too pleased with me for spending too much time cleaning and tidying up, and with all my efforts the cause of the smell remained a mystery.

Espinet 2 had been rafted up to the island pontoon and was the outermost boat, not far from the foundations of the quay. I was very surprised when another yacht moored against us. I was very concerned when its skipper ignored my warning, and the warning sign about the foundation rocks which was on the quayside. Later that evening, the yacht began to lean towards the quay as the keel grounded. The yacht was going to capsize onto the foundation rocks, causing serious damage. I lent the crew my spare fenders and told the crew how to position them and their own to form a cushion for the hull to rest on. This proved very difficult to do but, their efforts saved the hull from being damaged.

The following night a French yacht was moored against the quayside next to the warning notice. As the tide began to fall the yacht began to lean away from the quayside, and it was threatening to capsize onto the foundation rocks. The crew were eventually able to pull their yacht upright, with the aid of many lengths of rope; considerable manpower, and of course lots of shouting, which kept everybody awake.

The next yacht to come alongside the pontoon was a fabulous ketch, painted dark green, and you could shave in the reflection. The German owner of this fine yacht must have thought we looked half-starved, because he sent us a bucket full of freshly caught fish, together with his regards. Mary and I were delighted with our new neighbour's courtesy, and we decided to visit the beer keller, where we spent a memorable evening and ended our swing round the lamp post by dancing on the table.

The next morning I was still in a good mood, and as a result I let

Figure 28   *Espinet 2* and crew at peace.

our two Americans talk me into letting them continue with Mary and me, until we reached Roscoff. This was a decision which I later regretted, because they were very slow at keeping up with their payments into the communal kitty. Mary and I were having to make up the shortfall. I do hate mean people!

28 July 1975: Passage from St Helier to St Malo

With variable light winds and moderate visibility, we made slow progress until the wind settled to Force 2. With the spinnaker, genoa, staysail, and mainsail all set and nursed by the crew, we picked up speed, and the progress they had made since we left Plymouth pleased me no end. Disturbed currents and poor visibility made navigation and the final approach difficult once we reached Le Grand Jardin. Locking into the dock was hectic, and the tidal range is one of the largest in the world, so the lock is very deep. Once the lock gates opened the multitude of waiting boats crammed themselves inside so tightly there was hardly any space left to manoeuvre in. The exit from the lock was like the start of a Formula One race, as everybody rushed to find the best berth.

During our entire trip from St Helier, both hatches were kept open to ventilate the smell away. Drastic measures were called for as soon as possible after we had moored up, because the smell was so foul. I opened the seacock and flooded the boat to above the cabin floor level, I then closed the seacock and started to pump out the revolting bilge water, which had gone off because of somebody's vomit. Now we could enjoy our three-day break in our sweet-smelling accommodation.

My first visit to St Malo was back in 1947, when little remained of the old walled town except the mountains of reclaimed stone that was to be used in rebuilding the town, which had been totally destroyed by the Allies prior to the invasion of Europe, to prevent the Germans using the important port of St Malo. I enjoyed wandering along the old city walls and through the beautifully restored streets, with their houses and everything looking as though it had been scrubbed clean.

Watching the world go by whilst sitting outside a café with a nice cool drink is a fine way to spend an hour or so, but there are other outstanding attractions close by. Mont St Michel, which is a twin to St Michael's Mount in Cornwall, is well worth visiting, and all four of us enjoyed ourselves there.

It had been a very relaxing time and I felt in a holiday mood. The only downside to our stay was to see the crafty way the two Americans avoided their turns at the bar; when they were obliged to buy the drinks, they chose the cheapest, and when Mary and I were paying they chose only expensive drinks. The kitty was still running at a loss, although Mary always paid her share promptly. The meanness was getting me down, which was a pity because the cruise itself was going so well.

31 July 1975: Passage from St Malo to Lezardrieux

Forecast: ENE Force 3–5, moderate sea. Very poor visibility.

1020 hours: Locked out and set sail, but I soon realised just how dangerous it was going to be sailing in such poor visibility, with one of the world's greatest tides, many offshore rocks, and being without direction finder (DF) or Sat Nav. Dead reckoning is a very appropriate name for navigation, which sometimes is hit or miss. We managed to get an accurate fix at the Fairway buoy, and then another at Grand Legion, but after that the visibility was very poor for the rest of the passage.

Eventually I estimated that we were five miles from the Lezardrieux landfall when we caught sight of a yacht heading in our direction towards the approach, but we lost sight of it in the fog. We made our correct landfall but were too close for comfort, and we were being swept past the entrance of the river. However, our speed was a shade faster than the current, and we just made it into the safety of the river. By this time my nerves were rather frayed, having sailed almost blind for fifty-five miles in strong currents and fog, without DF, and near a very dangerous coast. We moored up in the marina for the night, thankful for having found it in the fog.

1 August 1975: Passage from Lezardrieux to Ile de Bréhat Isle and La Chambre

With little or no wind we motored down stream towards Le Chambre – our 'bedroom'. The rocks which we had passed on our way up the river at high water were well over thirty feet higher because it was now dead low water. We now had to make our way through the maze of rocks to reach La Chambre, and in one area there was only one foot between our keel and the rocks beneath. Navigation had to be spot on, so I checked and rechecked the data from the pilot guide before attempting to enter the lagoon which is called La Chambre, and is a well-known beauty spot, ideal for romantic nights spent sleeping under the stars.

The following day we set off to tour the Ile de Bréhat on foot. Returning from the tiring walk in the midday sun, Mary began to feel faint, so I walked with her at a slow place while the others walked ahead to the local café. At last! I thought, one of them is bound to arrive before us, and get a round of drinks in. If this happened it would be the first time since leaving Plymouth. No such luck, not even a glass of water for poor Mary! The boat's kitty still lacked their due contributions.

That evening while we were all enjoying our meal, an inflatable suddenly appeared from nowhere, filled with customs officers intent on pouncing on us. There must have been a change of plan, because they disappeared as silently as they came, leaving us wondering why they had made a beeline for us.

3 August 1975: Passage from Ile de Bréhat to Perros-Guirec

1225 hours. It was high tide when we started picking our way

Figure 29   *Espinet 2* at La Chambre.

between the rocks which had now shrunk by over thirty feet, and it was hard to believe that a rockscape could change so much. By the time we reached Petit Pen Azen beacon, the wind had freshened enough to make the rest of our journey both lively and pleasant. Having arrived at Anse de Perros, or rather the Bay of Perros, we

Figure 30   Mary on lookout.

93

found the lock gates of the marina were closed.

1905 hours: We dropped anchor in a sheltered area of the bay, and intuitively I laid out all the chain plus a long length of rope. In the middle of the night a violent wind shook the boat so hard we all woke up. I wondered if the anchor would hold, so I decided to open the fore hatch and shine our powerful torch onto the trip-line buoy, to see if it had shifted. I was unable to open the hatch because of the enormous wind pressure on it. A while later I tried again and managed to hold it for a few moments, just long enough to see that the rope and chain were bar tight. A strange rolling horizontal twister had hit us, and later we were told that it was a local phenomenon, but I have been told that it also occurs on the Lizard peninsula.

Locking into the marina was a bit hairy, because the sea rushes through the open lock at frightening speed, and once inside we could not find any indication of where to find the visitors' pontoon. I felt a right idiot roaming round the marina whilst a loudspeaker kept calling a strange word. We eventually found the visitors' pontoon, however, and we were soon reunited with our French friends from Guernsey.

We were promptly whisked away to their delightful home which overlooked the Bay of Perros, and we all freshened up with a shower. By the end of a sumptuous Breton meal, Mary and I felt we had been adopted into their extended family. Our hosts' generosity was overwhelming, and their kindness and friendship could not be faulted.

Each of us was asked to choose an activity we would like to do the following day. Mary and the others opted to spend their time in Lannion, which is an interesting period town, but I chose to visit the Sept Iles (Seven Isles) which lie to the north of Perros-Guirec. Jean, our host, said that would mean me locking out of the marina, so he offered to loan me his smallest yacht which he kept moored in the bay, and found two young friends to crew for me. I had a great time being chauffeured about, which made a change, and the Sept Iles were very interesting. Meanwhile the others found plenty to do in Lannion. Mary suggested that we would have to try and repay our hosts' hospitality, and an evening meal served aboard *Espinet 2* would be within our meagre budget.

Jean, his wife, their youngest son and his pal arrived for one of Mary's excellent on-board meals. Afterwards the youngsters asked permission to visit the local bar. Jean warned them not to get drunk, and off they went in search of younger company. The evening was a great success, but Jean was none too pleased when he could not find the youngsters. When he eventually found them drunk he was livid, because it is a social disgrace not to be able to hold one's drink, especially in public.

It transpired that the lads had met up with a yacht full of Welsh rugby players, who had challenged them to a drinking match. The French lads agreed on condition that they chose the drink. Distilled mead is of course illegal because of its potency, and it causes drunks to fall over backwards unexpectedly.

I saw one of the Welsh lads asleep on the road, with the taxis missing him near enough to give him a close shave. Another member of the team stood at the top of the ramp leading to our pontoon, and he was shouting out loud what he proposed to do to all the young women he could find. He then staggered along the pontoon. Mary said, 'For goodness' sake, see that he doesn't fall in, and you had better see that he gets back on board his boat.' Just as I offered to help him get back on board, he promptly lurched to one side and fell into the water. My reward for helping him get back onto the pontoon was for him to square up for a fight with me. He had no intention of returning to his boat unless I joined the party which was in full swing on board. I managed to dodge out of joining the rest of the drunks; once he went below, and returned to *Espinet 2* unharmed.

Mary and I were flabbergasted to see the Welsh crew smartly turned out and sober early next morning, as they did a turn of honour and waved goodbye.

The following day Mary was due to catch the Brittany ferry at Roscoff. She had been running short of cash, having had some of

Figure 31   Skipper and first mate.

her reserve disappear from its hideaway earlier on. She very kindly gave me her spare cash to help me on my way. It was such a pity that our passengers spoilt themselves by being so mean. They certainly enjoyed themselves during their eighteen-day cruise, which cost them about two pounds per day for the boat's kitty. I had enjoyed myself far more than I could have ever hoped, sailing with Mary as my first mate. I was sad to see her pass through customs at Roscoff on her way back to Plymouth and work.

Jean said that he would be failing as my friend if he let me sail single-handed to Brest, because the Breton coast is very dangerous. He kindly found two competent young sailors to crew for me, and who were willing to return to the UK with me if I needed their assistance. I thanked Jean and his wife for their outstanding hospitality and friendship. We agreed to meet up again, and we managed to meet again in Cornwall, back in Perros-Guirec, and in the South of France, where Mary and I lived when we retired.

6 August 1975: Passage from Perros-Guirec to Roscoff

Forecast: wind 3–2, ebb tide, visibility 10 miles.

1700 hours: Locked out of the marina with the two French lads as crew. They both handled the boat well, and set two head sails, main and spinnaker. Later on the wind died away, so we continued under engine. Shortly afterwards we caught up with a yacht drifting toward one of the many off-lying rocks, because they had run out of fuel for their outboard. We took them in tow and out of harm's way, until the wind picked up and they were able to go on their way again.

2245 hours: We arrived at Roscoff's port d'eaux profondes, where we anchored for the night, having covered a mere thirty-five miles. The good news was that we got on very well together as a team, and I was going to enjoy the rest of the journey to Brest with my crew doing all of the hard work, while I concentrated on navigation.

7 August 1975: Passage from Roscoff to L'Abervrach

Forecast: rain, moderate to poor sea state, fog.

We set sail under full main and number one head sail, in poor visibility. With the strong tides, the rugged coasts, and offshore hazards, my dead-reckoning navigation was going to be critical. At one time we were relying on the depth meter to give some advanced notice of breaking seas on the rocks, as the fog was too dense to see much further than our noses. At one time we came within little more than fifty metres of breaking seas on a rocky shore. The one-mile visibility in the approach to L'Abervrach, the fading daylight, and poor navigation lights made our landfall, and our way up to the marine, a nail-biting experience. However, we did have some onboard entertainment during the trip when Herve produced his Breton bagpipes, which he played very well, and they acted as a novel and effective foghorn.

Figure 32   A Breton piper on board *Espinet 2* en route to Brest.

8 August 1975: Passage from L'Abervrach to the commercial harbour in Brest

Forecast: wind NNW force rising, 3-mile visibility, sea moderate.

We left the mooring at 0930 hours and we were hoping for a good run to Brest, so I was surprised to find disturbed seas at the entrance to the aber (river mouth) and it looked as though there was a weather front approaching from the east. I was desperate to pass through the Channel du Four before it caught up with us, as it would put us in a very dangerous situation. By this time the wind had settled as a north-easterly Force 5 and rising. Benoit and Herve swapped the head sail for the spinnaker to increase our speed, as it looked as though we would have a fight on our hands if we were going to avoid a foul tide in the Channel du Four. The wind was increasing all the time, and the clouds began to look menacing, but

98

we maintained a good nine knots, so there was a chance we might win our race against the impending gale. We had been sailing 'on the edge' for the last half an hour so I told the lads that if the black clouds caught up with us, they must drop the spinnaker immediately. Both lads goaded me into keeping the spinnaker flying longer that I thought it prudent – they said that I was too old to handle the excitement.

In very agitated seas and the foul tide, the black clouds caught up with us as we almost reached the end of the Channel du Four, when a violent gust knocked *Espinet 2* down on her port side, with the cabin window under water. My cocky crew lost their self-confidence instantly, and clung on for dear life. Fortunately the spinnaker was just clear of the water. I grabbed the tiller and began paddling the rudder as hard as I was able to, so that the bows would turn to starboard. I shouted, 'As soon as she rises you must drop the spinnaker.' Slowly she began to rise and the crew realised that they were not going to drown, so they dropped the spinnaker and hoisted a small head sail in its place. We were nearly swept back up the Channel du Four during the knock down, and we only managed to claw our way against the foul tide and make our way towards the Commercial dock at Brest.

A later weather forecast had issued a gale warning for our area, and when we arrived in the dock, the harbourmaster instructed us to secure the boat with extra warps.

My friend from Perros-Guirec had given Benoit and Herve instructions to persuade me to return with them for a big wedding to which I had been invited, and he had given them enough money for the train fares. If, on the other hand, I was determined to sail back to Plymouth single-handed, he wanted the lads to introduce me to the owner of his favourite bar in town, and he would look after me while I remained in the area. I was sad to say goodbye to my two young friends. This was going to be my big chance to find out what real single-handed sailing was like on a long passage, and the chance to realise one of my ambitions.

9 August 1975: Lunchtime. Now on my own and feeling very

hungry, I wandered about until I found a popular restaurant. I was in luck because the food was excellent, and I soon made the acquaintance of two Frenchmen, one of whom was in charge of the massive dry dock in Brest. They had obviously been curious seeing a well-tanned visitor eating alone, and who was obviously a sailor. They were very interested in my sailing, especially my plans for returning single-handed, to my home port of Looe. The two friends both had the afternoon off work, so I invited them to join me in a twenty-four-mile trip to Châteaulin in the Rade de Brest. We all three enjoyed our jolly, and once again I found it very easy to make friends with sailors and other waterfront characters.

My entire evening was spent in Jean's bar, where the owner made sure that I was introduced to everybody, including the coxswain of the Ushant lifeboat, some dodgy IRA exiles, and a crowd of enthusiastic characters who were en route to the Lorient Folk Festival. At two a.m. it was too late for some of them to find accommodation, so I invited them to spend the night on board *Espinet 2*.

10 August 1975: One of Herve's friends appeared out of the blue, and was obviously hoping for a sail, so we visited Camaret, which is one of my favourite harbours. I was only too pleased to oblige as I had appreciated Herve and Benoit's company so much. That evening while I was crossing the foredeck of a large Edwardian gin palace, the owner invited me to join him on the bridge. He was very curious to learn what navigational equipment I had, and he was astounded to find I had so little. He also wanted to find out how I managed to do everything for myself. When someone else joined us, the owner recounted this fact again – how I managed to do everything myself, including navigation without the use of directional finding, self-steering, a log, and all the 'bolt-on goodies' which wealthy owners used. Unfortunately I had lots to do before I could set sail back home, and had to forego the pleasure of good company so that I could have an early night.

100

11 August 1975: Passage from Commercial Harbour, Brest to L'Aberildut

0930 hours: With little or no wind, strong adverse currents, and problems with the engine, I was unable to reach L'Abervrach, where I had intended to stay overnight. However, I just managed to reach L'Aberildut with only a little fuel left. Unfortunately there are no facilities whatsoever, and the nearest garage was a route march away carrying two American jerry cans. A motorist who filled up at the pumps took pity on me having to carry my cans all the way back to the boat, and gave me the most welcome lift I have ever had. I spent the rest of the evening making sure that everything was spot on for the long trip home. The one item missing from my wish list was self-steering, but as beggars can't be choosers, I was going to rely on myself steering instead.

12 August 1975: Passage from L'Aberildut to Looe, Cornwall

1345 hours: I left the mooring at very low water, and local knowledge was required, but my experiences on the upper reaches of the Helford River came to my rescue, and the keel never even touched bottom. Leaving France via the northern entrance of the Channel du Four in light and variable winds made progress very slow indeed. My final fix was the dipping distance and bearing of the Ile Vierge Lighthouse, at 1900 hours.

I managed to keep the boat on course, by balancing the genoa with the mainsail, and then lashing the tiller. This kept the boat on course for up to a quarter of an hour, but any changes in the boat's motion, or strange or different noises, would call for some adjustment in the gear. Variable north winds and regular tacking meant slow progress. I enjoyed sailing at night time, watching the stars instead of the compass most of the time, and once clear of the shipping lanes, I was able to cat nap, providing the wind was settled, and the boat kept itself on course. By mid-morning boredom and tiredness had set in, as I tried to coax the boat northwards with hardly any wind and even less fuel. Suddenly a submarine popped out of the sea as if by magic. It circled us while the crew on the conning tower watched me intently. Then it disappeared very quickly, leaving me wondering why *Espinet 2* had been checked out.

14 August 1975. 1245 hours: By this time the wind had picked up and good progress was made towards the Lizard peninsula, and as I drew nearer I spotted the main pack of the Fastnet race yachts, but the first two leading boats were well ahead. I fixed my position, and decided that I could manage to head off the pack. I arrived well ahead of the leading boats in the pack, and was able to remain there, much to my surprise. Just for a wind up, I arranged some washing on the rails, cooked a bacon-and-egg lunch which I ate slowly, read an old newspaper, and drank a cup of tea as the pack slowly gained on me by mere yards per minute.

The skippers of the leading boats were desperate to coax their uniformed crews to make every effort to overtake me, to avoid further embarrassment. Not a single word was spoken by any of the crews as they crawled past me at a snail's pace. A yacht which I had noticed further offshore altered course to intercept *Espinet 2* and came alongside to congratulate me on my sense of humour and skill, which had given him the best laugh he had enjoyed for ages.

By the time I had reached St George's Island off Looe, my brain and body had been running on empty for hours on end. I was in no state to steer a paddleboat across a pond, so I dropped the anchor and fell into a very, very deep sleep. Little did I know that I would be threatened with arrest when I tied up to the East Looe quay.

15 August 1975: With my yellow duster hoisted, I waited patiently for customs clearance. In the meanwhile word soon spread that *Espinet 2* had returned, and a small group gathered on East Looe quayside, curious to find out news of my adventure. Joe, a close friend of mine who had sailed with Paul and me to Ireland, was one of the first to seek me out. I waited for the local customs officer to give me my clearance, he was a man I knew well because I taught his son at the local comprehensive school. Naturally I was taken

aback when he became very officious. He demanded to know who the other person on board was, and what he was doing there. When I explained, he told Joe to get off the boat immediately. Joe took offence at his attitude, and was slow to move, whereupon I was cautioned that I would be arrested if he did not move straight away. Joe's leap was instantaneous, and it deprived me of the pleasure of seeing the inside of the police cell at the local nick.

In Retrospect

I enjoyed the challenge of single-handed sailing back from Biscay, although I was utterly exhausted by the end of the trip. Racing the Fastnet boats was the icing on the cake for me. I certainly did not feel lonely, and at times I felt the presence of somebody else beside me, just as I did when surfing the big waves off Rame Head and was thrown out of the cockpit in a near-fatal incident.

Coping with exhaustion in the open seas is far easier than being in the shipping lanes, sailing in dangerous waters, or trying to navigate when there are countless lights to identify, as there are in the Ushant–Brest area.

Self-steering, Sat Nav, and other bolt-on goodies are great if they work, but Sod's Law usually applies when they are needed the most. In severe weather conditions when the crew are usually at their lowest ebb, and even the engine does not work, knowing how to sail with only the bare essentials at hand can mean the difference between survival and disaster.

Living on board in cramped conditions brings out the best in some folk, and the worst in others. My advice to those contemplating cruising for any length of time is to see how you all get on together first. Before embarking on my first long cruise in *Espinet 2*, Joe and I took my girlfriend Mary for an offshore trip in rough conditions, and she impressed both Joe and me very much, as she continues to do after thirty years.

The reality of crossing the Atlantic was now a possibility as I had

Figure 33   Winter mooring at Forder.

a very seaworthy yacht, and some valuable experience to go with it. Sadly the logistics of entering the OSTAR did not add up, with the problem of taking leave of absence from teaching, and the funding of the enterprise, which meant that it could only happen when I retired. Nevertheless, I had another ambition, which was to sail to Portugal and back during my summer holidays in 1977.

16

Making Plans for the Cruise

Navigation. Compass deviation must be checked, to make sure that we did not wander off course and miss our landfall, as I did not fancy wandering about in the Atlantic if the log packed up. Charts had to be updated, especially the passage chart for crossing of the Bay of Biscay. At this stage of planning I could not expect to buy a direction finder, and I would need to economise by using my plastic sextant. Pilot guides and detail charts would be on my list of wants.

Passage details. My intention was to stop over in the commercial harbour at Brest, where we would take stock of our situation before continuing on our way across the Bay of Biscay, bound for Portugal. However, if there was any chance of meeting stormy weather en route, or if the crew were not up to the long crossing, Island hopping down the west coast of France to Spain would be a good alternative.

Crew. Paul, my son, had volunteered to act as first mate, but he would need to bail out within a fortnight in order to start work. Mary of course, was my permanent first mate and was available for the entire cruise. The one remaining vacancy was to be left open until the last week prior to the departure.

Finance. The cost of running the boat, and general house-keeping costs were to be shared, but the cost of our combined duty-free allowance was to be met by myself. Our entitlement would have filled the chain locker three times over, and made us chain-smoking alcoholics, and even with only one locker full of very cheap cigarettes and spirits, we could easily head in the same direction.

The ship's papers together with our passports, and providing sufficient funds for the trip, all needed to be reviewed.

The boat. A thorough check of all the standing and running rigging, battery checks, engine service, and shopping lists for perishable and non-perishable foods, sufficient fuel, gas cylinders, and personal items – all these had to be dealt with in the few days before departure.

A few days before we were due to sail, a friend of mine phoned me to say that Stan would like to join us for the entire cruise. I remembered having given him a three-hour lesson on board *Espinet* at Looe, for Sailing for Beginners. I did not know him well enough to take him on a long cruise, but I decided to take a chance that he would enjoy himself, and would be a suitable ship mate.

And so the summer cruise of 1977 began.

30 July 1977: Passage from Home Mooring to Millbay Dock, Plymouth

After collection of our duty-free from the bonded store, and with custom clearance and other formalities completed, we were at last free to set sail.

Passage from Millbay Dock, Plymouth, to Commercial Harbour, Brest

1400 hours: Forecast wind NNW 2–3, sea slight, visibility 30 miles. We set sail in high spirits for Brest, passing the Breakwater at 1400 hours, then we rounded Rame Head, under genoa, staysail, and mainsail, which were all filling nicely with a warm and friendly wind. With the compass heading set at 220 degrees we were starting our adventure.

1656 hours: Log 16.6 miles. Fixed position as we passed *Musketeer 2*, which was the replacement for *Musketeer*, the boat which I bought and renamed *Espinet 2*. From here our next sighting would be the Ushant Islands, so I would be calculating the tidal flow very carefully, and I would be keeping an eye on compass bearings which I fixed.

1755 hours: Forecast wind N 4–5, good visibility. Dropped staysail, and set course 225 degrees. We continued under jib only throughout the night, so that we could enjoy a leisurely and comfortable passage. We also maintained the same course throughout the night, to make the navigation for those on watch as simple as possible. The night watches were uneventful, so we all felt refreshed and looked forward to having our first sighting of the Ushant Islands. I was very relieved to find that Stan had enjoyed his first night at sea.

31 July 1977: 0800 hours. Ran the engine for a quarter of an hour to recharge both batteries, we then set the mainsail and started sailing in earnest. The visibility had now dropped to four miles.

1150 hours. Log 100 miles. Nothing to be seen! Are we just heading towards North America?

1515 hours. Shipping lane nearby, because we are hearing the thumping of heavy engines. Log now reading 114 miles, so we altered course to cross the lanes at right angles.

1655 hours. Entered the down channel lane. Log 120 miles. Fixed position on Le Stiff 190 degrees, and Roche Nividic 210 degrees. Changed course to pass Ushant to the west, and started motor sailing, in an attempt to avoid arriving at the Rade de Brest after dark. Unknown to me, our helmsman did not maintain the course which I had set during the time I was resting so that I would be alert enough for the run in through the countless navigation lights, strong currents, and overfalls. No wonder the big ships keep clear of this area if at all possible.

I became aware of a change of rhythm of the boat. Popping my head out of the hatchway, I saw to my horror that we were about to drop into a large hole in the severely disturbed sea beyond. I grabbed the helm and closed the throttle. We fell into the hole at six knots, and the nightmare of the dreaded overfalls began which I can recall in vivid detail after thirty years.

Having survived the ordeal at Ushant, I then had to cope with trying to identify all the relevant lights, in an area where the lights are more numerous than anywhere else in the world.

2 August 1977. 0430 hours: Arrived at the port of commerce, Brest, having sailed 176.8 miles in thirty-eight hours, at an average speed of 4.6 knots.

0900 hours: Mary was the only one on board who was firing on all four cylinders, so she volunteered to report to the harbour-master's office. In order to get ashore she had to climb the tallest ladder I have ever seen in a dockside, and the top rung was below the top of the quay. A very considerate gentleman, seeing an attractive lady in distress, pulled her to safety, thank goodness!

Mary returned with the bad news that there was a tropical cyclonic storm heading towards the west coast of France, and its arrival time was uncertain. This ruled out a direct crossing of the Bay of Biscay to Portugal. In the evening we decided to spend some time in the local dockland bar, so that we could decide on our change of plans for the rest of the cruise. We agreed that it would be prudent to daysail down the west coast, calling at some of the islands on the way to Spain. We could safely avoid the cyclonic storm catching us out by staying in the nearest harbour.

The bar turned out to be a very lively venue for all sorts of water-front characters, including a prostitute dressed in her traditional costume. We soon made friends with some youngsters, and we all

109

continued our partying on board *Espinet 2*, where our duty-free spirits proved to be very popular.

Unfortunately one of the lads sampled too many 'fisherman's champagne,' and finally he collapsed onto the steel decking of the barge next to us. The only way ashore was via a heavy plank which was fixed to a barge, and projected ten feet towards the dreaded ladder, which was set in a recess in the dockside.

After resuscitating the lad with black coffee, his friends decided to make him walk the plank propped up between two of them, but he then had to climb some forty feet of ladder, so one of the lads tied one of our mooring ropes under his arms with a bowline. He then went aloft with the lifeline to make sure that he remained on the ladder. All went well, and another friend mounted the ladder beside him just in case he let go, which he did two-thirds of the way up. The last I saw of him, he was being hauled up screaming in pain, until the soles of his shoes disappeared over the edge of the dockside. He left behind his jacket and address book, and he took with him Mary's pullover, and I hope some happy memories of his night out.

3 August 1977. Passage from port of commerce, Brest to Camaret

We had arranged to meet up with our new French friends who had partied with us the night before, but they must have had monumental hangovers to contend with because they missed our rendezvous. Our disappointment was compensated for by finding *Falmouth Packet* at anchor in the Camaret harbour, with a boatload of happy faces to greet us. It was a good opportunity to let Mary see over one of the Ocean Youth Club's ketches, and meet some of the crew. Our visit to *Packet* reminded me of my last trip on board her, when we had a very rough passage through the Channel du Four, with a crew of sixteen-year-old pupils, and the skipper ill with food-poisoning, as well as an essential sail change to cope with at the most dangerous section of the channel. It had been a genuine character-building event for some of the youngsters.

Figure 34 Bird's-eye view of Camaret which I photographed from the top of *Packet's* mast.

Figure 35 *Falmouth Packet*, mid-Channel meeting.

4 August 1977. Passage from Camaret to Audierne: The West Coast

We made an early start, and Paul was given the job of skippering for the day and having to choose the right time to pass through the Raz de Sein, which is a highly dangerous passage in bad weather.

111

Figure 36   La Belle Mary.

The tidal current is so strong that it can flatten seas caused by storms which are off the Beaufort scale. I was glad that Paul was showing up very well during his spell as Skipper, and I wondered if he would follow in his old man's footsteps.

We found a very pleasant spot moored up against the quayside right in the centre of town, and it gave us a chance to scrub *Espinet*'s bottom. We became a hazard to the taxis which hurtled past, so we moved out of harm's way, to the St Evette anchorage downstream, where we dropped anchor in deep water to avoid drying out.

The following evening we spent at a Fest Noz, listening to the mesmerising music, and watching the dancers perform the traditional dances in a strange trancelike manner. Returning to the boat in our rubber dinghy in the dark, Mary must have been affected by the strange music, because she was convinced that the tide had gone out, leaving her to climb much higher than she expected. It was quite a problem getting her back on board, and it was totally out of character to see her frightened.

5 August 1977. Passage from St Evette anchorage to Le Palais, Belle Ile

This passage turned out to be both pleasant and very relaxed, with the prospect of a three-day stopover in the wet basin at Le Palais, and out of harm's way of the threatened storm, but as far as I could make out there were no immediate signs of bad weather. We all decided to make the most of our mini-holiday.

Mary set to work buying fresh food from the market, and produced her best cuisine, considering it was cooked on a two-burner cooker, and the strange plumbing which caused the cold tap

Figure 37   Mary shopping at Belle Ile.

to pump out hot water from the engine's cooling system, when the cook least expected it. Mary always asked what time we expected to reach our destination, as she wanted to dish up the evening meal on time. Alas! This usually coincided with me trying to start the engine, and the fuel supply needed to be turned on under the only work surface, which was by that stage laden with hot, appetizing food, and nowhere to put it while the men tried to moor up.

Seeking revenge, and knowing that I suffered from vertigo, she persuaded us to visit a tall lighthouse, where she forced me to go outside the lantern and stand and look down at the view below. This was pay-back time for the many times I had frightened the living daylights out of her at sea. My dose of vertigo was a fitting punishment, but she more than made up for it by keeping us all very well fed. All good things come to a end, and we had to swap our brief holiday on Belle Ile for sailing southwards again for fifty-six miles to Ile d'Yeu.

8 August 1977. Passage from Le Palais, Belle Ile to Port Joinville, Ile d'Yeu

We set sail at 1100 hours, which was late in the day to fight head winds and strong adverse currents, with only the engine to help us make headway. Late in the afternoon the wind settled from the west, so we managed to conserve our meagre fuel reserve. We were unable to lock in to the dock at Port Joinville, so I chose to anchor offshore between a coaster and a yacht, because both of our batteries were nearly flat and would not be able to keep our riding light going all night.

During the night the entire fleet of small single-handed fishing boats hurtled past us, as though they were being driven by Formula One racing drivers at the start of a Grand Prix. I awoke to find that our borrowed riding lights had disappeared, together with the coaster and the yacht. The wash from each of the fishing boats tossed us about; as they passed us with only a few metres to spare,

114

and the laughter of these lunatics could be heard echoing across the water for ages. This was the first time we were to experience first hand the west coast fishermen's dislike of yachtsmen, and also to hear that they regard their waters as their own domain. Under the circumstances we thought it would be prudent to make an early start if we hoped to do some shopping at the next port of call. Paul would leave the boat, to hitchhike back to Roscoff to catch the Brittany ferry to Plymouth, because he was due to start work again. The remainder of the crew would miss his sense of humour, his company, and his help.

9 August 1977. Passage from Port Joinville, Ile d'Yeu, to Les Sables d'Olonne

Les Sables d'Olonne is situated some thirty miles away on the west coast. With little or no wind, and hardly any fuel, it was going to be a sailing passage only. The good news was the sunshine which sparkled on the sea, and made sunbathing a must for the crew. I was voted helmsman for the trip, so that the lazy b.....s could toast themselves. The large spinnaker was ideal for putting them in the shade when I wanted to wind them up.

The wind strengthened as we approached the coast, doubling our speed to eight knots, but it looked as though we would have to drop the spinnaker as we rounded the headland, and then hoist the genoa. Much to my surprise, the idle sunbathing crew leapt to their feet and changed sails quicker than I expected.

As we turned the corner we found the bay was filled with very rough water, which was covered with a layer of 420s racing hell for canvas, and blocking our way towards the harbour mouth. Our idle sunbathing crew had suddenly become real professional sailors and with their help we carved our way through the entire fleet, to the dismay of the skippers as we took the wind out of their sails, one after another. I was very impressed both with *Espinet*'s performance and with my seamanlike crew.

The harbourmaster at Les Sables d'Olonne turned out to be a real gem when he tried to find the charts which we needed for the rest of our cruise to Spain. Unfortunately they were not to be found locally, and there was no further information about the arrival of the long-awaited cyclonic storm. Paul started hitchhiking to Roscoff, which turned out to be a very unpleasant ordeal.

Mary has the personality and natural charm to make friends anywhere, and Jeff and Audrey, our quayside neighbours, fell for her charms straight away. We all enjoyed a musical evening in town, and afterwards we agreed to meet up in La Rochelle's town centre marina. On our last night spent moored next to *Touchdown*, our new friend's boat, the snoring was accompanied by a tune on the forestay, so perhaps there was going to be some real wind before long.

11 August 1977. Passage from Les Sables d'Olonne to La Rochelle

1115 hours. We set sail along the coast as I decided to pass between the Ile de Rey and the mainland where the depth of water is very small at low tide, especially in Pertuis Breton. We did not run aground, and we made it to our rendezvous to find that we had lost *Touchdown* en route. However, we had chosen a superb location for our stopover, and we were going to make the most of it. Still no warning of the storm reaching Biscay, and we had no luck in finding the charts and pilot guide.

12 August 1977. The Customs Officer Gets His Man

The quayside offers lots of interesting things to see, and we all made the most of our time wandering round the old town, which surrounds the harbour, and soaking up the atmosphere, as well as some brandies and coffee. I suggested that we should check out the dock which is situated on the other side of the harbour, to find out if it was possible to stay there, as it was only possible for visitors to remain in the town centre marina for up to four days.

We were admiring the expensive yachts moored up with their sterns facing the quayside, but anchored some distance from it. A customs officer asked the sole person on board one of these posh boats to bring his very upmarket craft close enough to the ladder so that he could collect the crew's passports and ship's papers for processing. The arrogant wealthy owner refused to do what he had been politely asked to do. Later in the day we happened to be passing when the owner asked the officer when the passports would be returned. He replied in perfect English, 'I quite understand how anxious you are to sail today, but unfortunately the office is now closed for the weekend, and it is such a pity that you will be delayed for two days.' The owner's arrogance deflated like a pricked balloon, to the amusement of the bystanders.

13 August 1977. *Espinet 2* was still moored in the marina with the crew enjoying their mini-break, but I was concerned that I could not find the elusive charts for the area south of the Gironde, nor a pilot guide for the northern coast of Spain. It appears that the French are not keen to venture into the lower part of the Bay of Biscay. At the time I wondered why, but we were destined to find out the hard way.

Finally *Touchdown* arrived, having been delayed by her owners visiting the Ile de Ré. Both Jeff and Audrey were very keen for us to accompany them, and follow the sun to Spain, making for San Sebastien directly. I pointed out that I only had the Biscay passage chart, and had no pilot guide for the area. Jeff brushed my problems aside, saying that I could copy the necessary details from his own guide for the landfall and the approach to the harbour, which is situated in the Bay of San Sebastien. He also said that they would come alongside every two hours, so that he could give me our latitude and longitude. The most recent weather forecast gave no warning of any impending storm. However, the evening sky foretold severe weather for the next day. My gut instinct was to

THE UPS AND DOWNS OF SAILING

delay our departure. I also pointed out that our fuel range was very limited, and that his ketch was much larger and faster than *Espinet 2*. He kindly offered to give us a tow if necessary.

The die was now cast, and we agreed to sail the next morning. I did not sleep well because I kept trying to remember when I had last seen such a dramatic-looking sky, and what had followed it. Dante's 'Inferno' came to mind, and I regretted leaving my camera at home.

14 August 1977. Passage from La Rochelle to San Sebastien, Spain. Biscay

0645 hours: *Touchdown* and *Espinet 2* set sail, in good conditions, but with only a slight easterly wind to help us on our way. Jeff gave us a tow to help us conserve our fuel. The mid day forecast gave a wind shift to south-east 2–3, rain, sea poor, fog. We had already parted our tow and were sailing with the genoa and mainsail at a good speed. Somehow I did not believe the wind would remain moderate for the remainder of the passage, bearing in mind Nature's warning of those dramatic clouds. Jeff had kept his word about giving us an accurate fix every two hours, which left me with little navigation to do, except for recording the log, time and course. Mary and I had enjoyed a romantic night, watching the stars and basking in the warm night air.

15 August 1977. Position estimated 44 deg 54 mins North, 41 mins West.

0400 hours: Everything began to change. The wind had been easterly for eight hours, but it then swung one hundred and eighty degrees and became Force 4 westerly. By this time I was convinced that we had at last been caught out by the cyclonic storm which we had been warned of so long ago. The Atlantic swell increased in length, the sea state was already poor and the visibility was falling all the time. *Touchdown* was pulling ahead, even with us racing as fast as possible with the genoa still set. I could feel in the air that this was going to be a severe storm, and an electrical one as well.

0810 hours: The thunderstorm was in full swing, and the conditions in every respect were going downhill rapidly. I made the decision to drop the genoa if the wind increased, which meant that we would lose contact with *Touchdown*. The visibility was very poor indeed, and we had not been given our position for almost ten hours. Navigation was now going to be a nightmare if we couldn't get sight of one of the lighthouses.

0830 hours: We had now reached the stage when racing through heavy seas and grossly over-canvased with the wind rising was downright dangerous. I told the crew to be prepared to drop the genoa at a moment's notice. We had by now lost contact with our friends, and there was no possibility of finding them and getting our position pinpointed. I nervously continued to look upwind into the fog, in case a 'white-out' approached.

0900 hours: All hell was let loose when the fog upwind turned white, and began to scream in anger. Mary and Stan manhandled the genoa with great fortitude, and just managed to bundle it below and lock the fore hatch, as the wall of solid spray driven by a most violent wind, struck our port side. I had sheeted in the mainsail as hard as possible, to minimise any damage caused by gybing. Within seconds, I realised that rounding up to go head to in such a violent wind could well bring down the mast, leaving us in a hopeless situation in the middle of the Bay of Biscay at the mercy of a tropical cyclonic storm.

I decided to run before the wind to reduce its velocity, but what followed was the ride of my life, or rather the ride for our lives. The wind was even stronger than I had bargained for, and the sea was as rough as rats, making it extremely difficult to avoid a gybe. The boat was now unbalanced with only the mainsail set, so the bow was very close to going under! Without warning a huge wave broke against our stern, with such force that it picked us up and catapulted *Espinet 2* clear of the water, and for some moments we were flying with our keel twelve feet above the water. A memorable splashdown followed. The ferocious wind and breaking seas now seemed determined to drive us under, and if I lost control for even a moment a fatal broach would capsize the boat.

I now carried the responsibility for the lives of my friends, and I was at fault for not paying attention to the message which the sky had given before we set sail, and for not having confidence in my own judgement, instead of being persuaded otherwise by Jeff.

Gradually the foam-covered seas gave way to less dramatic ones, and the visibility improved, giving us a spectacular panorama for God to display his fireworks, which consisted of shooting stars and thunder and lightning. The wind gradually slackened to thirty-something knots, and later it disappeared completely, leaving the burgee hanging limp for a quarter of an hour, so we were in the eye of the storm at 1500 hours.

During the previous twelve hours when the storm was at its most violent stage, navigation had simply been to keep our true course of 180 degrees, so I was desperate to fix our position from the Biarritz and the San Sebastien lighthouses. When the visibility improved dramatically I saw the first flashing light, which I reckoned just had to be the Biarritz light. However, I was never able to identify it because it kept disappearing behind the massive swell, and was also obscured by the constant lightning.

Both batteries had been flat, so we ran the engine during our passage through the eye of the storm, but even the engine failed, and to make matters worse our torch gave up the ghost and we now had to rely on an antique student candle lamp to illuminate the chart, compass and the cabin. We were without navigation lights. Eventually the sweep of a lighthouse's beam caught my eye, and I assumed it to be the Higuer Lighthouse, at San Sebastien. It was dead ahead but a long way off. My fix on these two lights confirmed that we were still on course, but we would arrive after dark, at our final destination. However, I was not happy about the inadequate information which I had copied from Jeffry's pilot guide and chart for our landfall and the approach to the harbour. I intended to lay off shore until first light, as the coastline, which is some thousand feet high in places, obscured everything in total blackness, including the city and its bay.

Mary and Stan had other ideas because they were tired out, and fed up with the stress of 'living on the edge', and were desperate to be tucked up in their bunks and safe in harbour. Against my better judgement, I was persuaded to attempt the approach.

I remembered that leading lights had to be followed, when passing through the very narrow gap to enter the Bay of San

Sebastien, so I was very relieved to see some ahead. I decided to approach them very cautiously. I watched the depth meter, which indicated a rise and fall of the swell to be in excess of thirty feet, and the sea bed was rising very rapidly. The shape of a coaster became clearer, together with a promenade, and some street lights and traffic lights. The coaster turned out to be a wreck which was high and dry on the sandy beach, and my leading lights were only traffic lights. By this time we were only a short distance from the huge seas breaking on the foreshore. We would be joining the coaster if I did not react quickly enough and get into deeper water. As we pulled away from the shore, we were very surprised to a see a large fishing boat nearby, so I decided to approach it close enough that I could ask them in which direction we must go to find the entrance into the Bay of San Sebastien. However, it was impossible to get close enough to be heard properly, so I resorted to sign language. The crew must have realised where we wanted to go, and directed us to the west.

Journey's End. St Sebastien, Spain

Having been pointed in the correct direction, we set off along the coast in pitch blackness, and kept a constant watch on the depth of water to make sure we did not end up on the rocks. A while later we were rewarded by finding the V-shaped opening and beyond the blaze of the city lights, which surrounded the welcome bay. Sailing through the narrow gap, with the angry seas crashing into the rocks, which were within a stone's throw, at night-time in such bad conditions was enough to spook the best helmsman. It was no thanks to Jeffry's pilot guide that we had found our way to the safety of a mooring close to the beach. Having tied up to the unoccupied buoy, we all crashed out without even making a well-deserved hot drink.

Not long afterwards, Mary woke me to say that an armed member of the Civil Guard had come on board to question me. This officer only spoke the Basque language. I tried speaking French and Mary tried her Spanish without any reaction from him, which made the interview ridiculous. After inspecting our passports and finding that we had sailed all the way from Plymouth, he departed, leaving us to fall asleep like three snoring corpses. It later transpired that Don Carlos had just taken up residence for the summer here. We remained under close surveillance for the duration of our stay, in case we turned out to be Basque terrorists.

Unfortunately our sleep was once again disturbed, but this time it was caused by a very irate owner of a motor-cruiser who demanded that we vacated his mooring immediately. We hurriedly departed in a state of disarray and still in our pyjamas, to the accompaniment of a chorus of loud Basque voices. We soon found our way into the harbour where we moored up, safely for the rest of the night, still in our pyjamas. We fell into our bunks exhausted and slept like logs. Even the sound of our snoring sounded like sawing wood!

Refreshed by our well deserved sleep we were anxious to to visit the Royal Sailing Club of San Sebastien where we hoped to shower and find some decent food. This necessitated inflating the rubber

122

dinghy in order to cross the harbour and save a long detour. Much to our delight a boatman insisted that he rowed us to the other side, because he said that it was unladylike to use the rubber dinghy. He then directed us to the club where we assumed he was employed ferrying the club members to their boats.

With such an efficient service I was optimistic about our reception at the club. The Steward was very obliging and directed us to the bar where we could find bar snacks. However, the well dressed club members were not impressed by our salt stained attire, and they ignored us, but we were not put off and we fortified ourselves with the free melt-in-a-moment goodies and chilled drinks. Mary plucked up courage to ask the steward where we could watch some Flamenco dancing. This apparently was a faux pas because the Basques are very anti-Spain and its culture. Nevertheless, the steward grabbed hold of Mary, and they both gave a very professional demonstration of Flamenco, much to the disapproval of the female club members. We retired from the frosty atmosphere at the club without showering.

It transpired that our boatman was the harbour nightwatchman who had admired Mary for having crossed the Bay of Biscay in such bad weather, and of course her natural charm. We all three of us made friends with him, although we had no common language between us. One day he invited us into his office, but he closed the shutters in case the Secret Service man overheard his conversation. He then recounted how the 'State' dealt with Basques who stepped out of line, with machine guns! Our next visit to the office was for afternoon tea, or rather for wine, fruit and cakes which his wife had provided for us.

All the tuna boats had already returned to harbour before we arrived because of the storm, and they remained in harbour for the rest of our time in Spain. Each day we were warned not to sail because of the katabatic winds which are of gale-force strength, so we decided to make the most of our stay in this charming city.

Surprise, surprise! *Touchdown* came alongside, and Audrey's greeting was to point to the heavens and shout, 'All this and pissing rain.' They had been delayed because when they arrived, just before we had, they had anchored behind the island in the bay for shelter from the storm. They found it too dangerous to leave the anchorage, or to use their dinghy, so they remained stuck fast for two days.

That evening we were invited to step aboard for a combined meal. However, this was easier said than done because of the violence of the wind and the roughness of the water inside the dock. It made me think that we were still in the middle of the storm and out at sea. The evening was a great success, but it now looked that we would be returning to the UK as soon as the weather improved because our schedule was very tight. Our friends, however, planned to continue further westwards along the Spanish coast.

Next day they collected a gas cylinder before visiting the main post office. They were frog-marched outside by armed policemen, who thought that they were Basque terrorists intent on blowing up the building. We also had a problem with our own bottle gas, which needed an adaptor so that we could use continental-type cylinders.

Fortunately one of the policemen understood our problem, and told us to follow him, saying that he would point us to a shop that sold camping gear. It did not stock the adaptor, however, so we were then directed out of town to another shop. When we arrived at our destination there was only a barber shop, so Mary showed the barber the address and asked in sign language where it was. This led to the barber and his clients, including a partly shaven one, to debate on the pavement, as only the Latins can, where the shop might be. The half-shaven client concluded the debate by telling us we had got off the bus one stop too early. We finally procured the adaptor and decided to celebrate its purchase by visiting a fishing port situated some twenty-five miles to the west.

Next morning we set off towards town, and on the way I asked a charming elderly gentleman where the bus station was, and which bus should we take. He then said that we should follow him and he would put us on the correct bus. However, neither he nor any of the waiting passengers could make their minds up as to the correct bus for taking us to our fishing port. The outcome of all the deliberations was that we had a tour of a cement works and a very dusty village, instead of our picturesque fishing village.

Our next attempt to travel to our destination was by way of the train, but the man at the ticket office refused point blank to issue the tickets and he insisted that no trains ran to such a place. By this time I was beginning to lose my temper, but I was very surprised at what my raised voice and sign language could achieve when we had the support of a sympathetic audience. Our tickets appeared as if by magic, and we were on our way. Our journey in the pre-Civil War rolling stock was a never-to-be-forgotten experience, as our carriage swayed and rattled so much that it was a wonder it remained on the rails. Whilst having a pee through a round hole in the floor of the WC, which was supposed to be the urinal, I put my hand on the side of the carriage as the train lurched as it swung round a bend. The side of the train separated from the floor, leaving a good four-inch gap. I knew then that the ticket clerk must have had serious concerns for our survival, or must have been so embarrassed by the state of the track and the rolling stock that he was reluctant to sell us the tickets. The slatted wooden seats left their marks on our backsides for the rest of our day.

The charms of the quaint fishing village and its quayside were enhanced by the welcome smell of chargrilled sardines. We had reached our destination at last and all in one piece, but many a trainspotter would have paid good money for a ride on such an ancient line. The downside to our visit was that there were no shops, cafés or restaurants open, and no public transport available to take us the twenty-five miles back to our floating flat. With a shortage of cash, we were obliged to walk in the blistering heat as far as possible, but we finally gave in and found a taxi to take us back to the boat.

Touchdown had left the quayside, and in its place we found four French lads who had borrowed one of their father's yachts, and had ignored the restriction which the owner of the yacht had made about not sailing in bad weather. They were very impressed to find that we had sailed from La Rochelle in the storm. We soon made

125

friends with the lads, who all had a great sense of humour. They made us promise to call on them at Capbreton on our way home if we had enough time.

The strong winds persisted, and no signs that they would improve, so on the fourth day I decided to walk to the headland to see for myself what the conditions were like out at sea. I concluded that providing we could make a five-mile offing, it would be safe enough to visit the first harbour to the east, or even further on.

26 August 1977: Our passage was to break loose from being storm-bound in San Sebastien.

We set sail in a strong northerly head wind, rough seas, a very large swell and good visibility. A group of ocean racers had set off before us, and this boosted my confidence in my judgement.

To force our way through the very narrow entrance and into the Bay of Biscay necessitated having maximum power, so we motor sailed under working canvas. Tacking out through the narrow entrance required nerves of steel, because the large breaking seas were very close to us. I can still remember the crowd of onlookers staring at *Espinet 2* from the viewing platform high above us, with the seas surging towards them, as they followed our little drama.

Once clear of the land, we faced mammoth-sized swells, and very rough seas in every direction. As the ocean-going racing yachts sailed westwards they kept disappearing in the swell, as we kept tacking further offshore. By the time we had made a five-mile offing, the wind had increased to full gale force, and the seas were getting even rougher. It was now 'Make your mind up time, Bishop'. Without any detailed data about the harbours to the east it would be foolhardy to do anything other than return to San Sebastien. The devil you know is better than the one you don't is very good advice, so we turned tail and ran back.

I needed to remain at the helm, and could not risk asking either Mary or Stan to do a sail change because the boat was being thrown about so violently, and I feared that there was a real chance someone could be injured, or be lost overboard. We learned later that while we were sailing offshore, one of the ketches lost its

126

rig. It must have taken a very violent wind to have brought down its main mast, and we had been out in similar conditions.

The spectacle of the thousand-foot coastline disappearing each time we reached the bottom of the great swell, with a backdrop of the high mountains dominating the skyline, was memorable to say the least, and the five-mile ride over the rough watery hills was an exciting experience. However, it was the run through the narrow entrance to the San Sebastien Bay which gave the crowd who had gathered to watch *Espinet 2* make her dramatic passage through the hell hole to safety something to remember.

Our feelings of relief were short-lived, because we were unable to find any shelter in the lee of the island, where I had planned for Mary and Stan to drop sails. The gale was now reaching its climax, so I decided to make a dash for the outer tidal basin and drop the sails inside. I told Mary and Stan that it was of the utmost importance that they had to be ready with the fenders, and the sails had to be dropped the moment I gave the sign. My first sighting of the basin was of utter chaos, and the only option we had was to come alongside a large motor cruiser which was being held off by numerous warps. We managed to tie up alongside without causing any damage, other than making my blood pressure rise and giving the cruiser's owner a near heart attack when he saw our approach. There was a high degree of desperation as the boat owners and their crews tried to prevent their craft from being smashed into match wood by the violent gusts of wind and the bathtub sloshing water inside the basin itself.

We should have waited for the conditions to improve to less than gale-force 8.

27 August 1977: The weather at last showed signs of improvement, so we shopped in town for supplies of food, and also for water, gas and fuel, which was readily available on the quay. Later in the day another British yacht came alongside the quay, and its owner, in a very self-opinionated manner and voice, demanded to be refuelled. Nothing happened. The owner became irate when nobody appeared at his bidding. What a difference to the reception

our boatman had given us. We watched the arrogant man's face become even more purple for a while, but we never found out if his boat was refuelled.

Mary, who has some Spanish, was curious about a man who was always hanging about on the quay, and when she had asked him the way to town on the day we arrived, he gave her the instructions in Spanish in a most polite manner. Throughout our stay we all wondered what he was doing. The day of our departure he said in perfect English that he hoped we had enjoyed our stay, and wished us a safe journey home. He was in fact a secret agent who had been keeping us under surveillance!

28 August 1977. Passage from San Sebastien to Capbreton. Return to France

0830 hours: We sailed out of the harbour under genoa and mainsail, with offshore winds, and oh what a joy it was to have a soldier's wind, sunshine and tranquil waters.

1300 hours: With St Jean de Luz abeam we started tacking, but with only Force 1–2 northerlies, our progress was painfully slow.

1630 hours: Off l'Ardour channel the sea changed to the deepest blue Imaginable, and we were still topping up our tans.

2100 hours: We picked up plastic on the propeller during a difficult entry into Capbreton at dead low water. The engine cut out at a critical moment, just as we began searching for a vacant berth in the marina, but by now the crew had become proficient so we came to no harm. Without the continuous gale-force winds to worry about, we put ourselves and *Espinet* to bed, having enjoyed our first real sunshine for fifteen days, and now without the worry, we could sleep easy.

Sometime during the night we were disturbed by French voices. 'Yes they have arrived, but it is too late now, so we will see them in the morning.' The voices were familiar – it was the lads from San Sebastien.

Our Day Out

Next morning the four lads arrived, having borrowed two cars from their parents, and with our day's schedule planned, which they had carefully thought out. Our first item on their agenda was a guided tour and shopping at Bayonne. Next we were off to the finest seafront restaurant in Biarritz. The lads told the head waiter that they had clubbed together to give us something to remember them by. The head waiter produced chilled quality wine and served us with kir at the very best table, which had a stunning view of the Spanish coast. We then spent our evening in the marina night club at Capbreton. What fantastic courtesy and friendship from these young men!

The following day we wandered down to the harbour entrance to see what the conditions were like out at sea, for our exit the following day. The river entrance is protected by two long sea walls which stretch straight out into the sea, and perched on their ends are small lighthouses. An enormous quantity of water flows in and out of the river mouth with each tide, making it very difficult to exit when there is a head wind and a flood tide. Imagine our amazement when we saw a large catamaran appear through the curtain of surf which was higher than these small lighthouses! The skipper struggled to keep on course, because the ocean surges were lifting the craft up to ten feet above the roadway where we were standing, yet none of the water spilt onto the road. I wondered what was in store for us when the time came for us to leave. In the afternoon Stan and I helped an Englishman and his wife moor up his boat with little more than a short length of washing line. They had actually come to the end of their tether after a long cruise which was obviously going to end their marriage.

Stan and I returned to *Espinet 2* only to find that Mary had been chatted up by a high-ranking army man, who kept his wee boat for just a little fishing. I am sure that he would have liked to set sail with Mary, but he settled with inviting the three of us for cocktails that evening. His wee boat was in reality a fantastic 'gin palace', which he used for tuna fishing hundreds of miles out in the Atlantic Ocean. His three permanent crew kept the vessel ready for him when he arrived in his own aircraft from Paris for some relaxation.

Our meeting that evening was most fortunate for me, because he explained that our return passage to Arcachon the next day would pass through a 2,400-square-mile firing range. It was vital to know which parts of the range were in use, if we hoped to avoid being bombed, shelled or missiled. He thoughtfully called up the control centre for the necessary information. We all enjoyed the cocktail party, and Mary looked as though she was very much at home in the sumptuous salon, with its pale grey pigskin-upholstered armchairs, whilst Stan and I were rather 'below decks'.

30 August 1977: Passage from Capbreton to Arcachon

Our first attempt to leave harbour was a failure due to fouling the propeller with plastic. I cleared it by diving beneath the boat from the rubber dinghy three times. I just hoped that I did not have to clear the prop out at sea, because I doubted that I could manage to cut through the tough plastic in rough water.

However, I had not realised that a permanent trail of rubbish had to be sailed through, and it stretched for many miles along the Les Landes coast. Crossing it to gain the open sea was a nightmare, but we managed to avoid a forty-foot tree and some other large pieces of debris, but we finally snagged some plastic, which I cleared by putting the engine in reverse and avoided having to dive beneath the rubbish to clear the propeller.

We followed the sandy beach which stretches all the way north to Arcachon, which is the only harbour between the Gironde and Capbreton. All went well for the next sixty miles as we kept in the safety zone, which is a five-mile strip close to the sandy beach. We all enjoyed watching the tourists enjoying their sunny beach holidays. As we came to the end of the firing rage, sea mist began to settle, giving about a quarter of a mile visibility. Mary suddenly

130

said, 'Can you hear that noise?' I replied, 'Don't worry, it is only the sails flapping.' I listened for a few moments. My God, it is gunfire! I thought – and it seemed to be directed at us. I started the engine and we scuttled away as fast as possible. We never actually saw the naval vessel appear through the mist, but its guns certainly put the wind up us, because when Mary had asked the army officer if any boats had been sunk by the firing, he said that only one yacht had been sunk and another had its mainsail holed the previous year... Was he pulling her leg at the time, I asked myself!

We found the landfall buoy with some difficulty in the poor visibility – it was much further offshore than I had imagined.

It is forbidden to enter the complex channel itself at night, and during daylight each of the numbered buoys must be recognised in turn before proceeding to the next. Sailing along the tortuous channel was like being in a maze, with walls of breaking surf reaching above the top of our mast, or like being on a winding path of cobbled waves.

Figure 38   The sandbanks extend beyond the ones shown here at high tide.

Having successfully avoided being shelled from the firing range, we came under fire from potato-throwing fishermen who believed that their patch should be yacht-free. I made a mental note that it would be impossible to exit the channel in bad onshore weather and with a foul tide.

With only twenty-four hours to spare from our tight schedule, it was important that we stocked up again. However, Mary found time to return the potatoes to the fishermen, leaving them with egg on their faces.

The huge sand dune which towers above the town is taller than St Paul's Cathedral, and is some place to surf-board down. It was such a pity that we did not have the time to try our hand at the young-sters' sport. The large tidal lake is home to the famous oyster farms, and there are interesting nooks and crannies along its edges. One day I would like to spend some quality time in the area.

1 September 1977. Passage from Arcachon to La Rochelle

We departed from the town pier and motor sailed towards the channel at 1700 hours. We were obliged to motor sail, and to take advantage of the slacker water on the inside of the bends, in order to make progress against the very strong current all the way to the landfall buoy. The conditions out at sea were excellent, so we settled down to enjoy a welcome meal, and later we savoured the aroma of the warm night air. The stars were very bright, and without the moonlight it appeared that God had polished them for the occasion.

Keeping watch for shipping during the night, I spotted a mast-head light astern of us, but many miles away. Gradually it appeared to be catching up with us, but I found it very strange that there were no port or starboard lights showing. I considered altering course to avoid being run down. Suddenly it dawned on me that the mysterious vessel had only been a rising star. My mind had been switched off by the prolonged gentle motion of the boat, the warmth of the night air, and the lack of any other light. Exhaustion on some rare occasions has played havoc with my reasoning in the same way.

2 September 1977. As we approached La Rochelle late in the afternoon we caught sight of a wrecked coaster perched on rocks some miles offshore which we had passed on our way to Spain. Imagine our surprise to see that a good-sized fishing boat was lying wrecked on top of it.

We arrived at La Rochelle Town Centre marina at 2005 hours, after logging 118 miles of delightful cruising, and having strangely lost one sock and one pillow en route. We all decided to rest up the next day, and then spent a few hours in town before heading north again. The waterfront café which we had chosen was an ideal spot to watch the world go by. However, the town's tearaways spent their time driving their motor scooters in and out of the tables in front of our café. The brandies and coffee which I drank soon made me light-headed, but Stan was loath to take to the sea again, so he plied me with another. I foolishly expected the night air to sober me up.

What I had forgotten was the lack of moonlight, and the channel buoys were unlit, so it was exceedingly difficult to find them. I was too drunk to negotiate the inshore passage between the Ile de Rez and the mainland because it is shallow in places. I was obliged to go all the way round the island. Beating to windward in rough seas without enough wind to drive us through the waves made Stan and me very queasy.

Mary went on strike and refused to make us hot drinks because she was so angry at us being drunk. To make matters worse, we met one of those fishermen who decided to give us the run about by changing course to wrongfoot me. However, I had sobered up by this time and we avoided him without too much trouble. Mary reminds me from time to time, of the skipper of *Espinet 2* who was drunk in charge of his boat. At least we arrived safely, which is more than I can say about the pilot of a Brittany ferry who rammed it into the buffer when docking at speed, because he was drunk.

Les Sables d'Olonne

At the end of our eight-hour trip, both Stan and I had dried out, but Mary was still not on talking terms with a pair of drunks. The atmosphere on board remained chilly, so Stan and I went into town for a strong coffee, without the brandy. On our return to the boat Mary was not in a good mood and even mentioned that she would prefer to return home by public transport. Fortunately she thawed out and became her usual loveable self.

5 September 1977: Passage from Les Sables d'Olonne to Ile d'Yeu.

0930 hours: We completed the modest thirty-four miles to our next stopover in sunshine, head winds, and good spirits. Not brandy this time! As we approached the dock gates at Port Joinville at low water, we went aground, much to the amusement of the local youths. The town itself reminded me of the Wild West, but with the gangs riding bareback on scooters instead of horses.

6 September 1977: Passage from Ile d'Yeu to Belle Ile

0930 hours: We left the inner harbour after having a poor night's sleep, due to the rowdy youngsters who had camped out for the night close to us. Although the head winds persisted for the whole day, the sea was moderate, visibility good and it was sunny. We averaged four knots and arrived at 2330 hours in the wet basin at Le Palais at Belle Ile.

The following day, Stan sorted out the engine's problem of fuel starvation. Mary and I visited the market to stock up with fresh produce, and to have an extended coffee break on our own. Mary as usual produced a first-class meal in the evening, and we decided to catch up with our lost sleep at Port Joinville. Alas! We were woken at closing time at the bar close to us on the quay, by what sounded like heavy rain falling on our coach roof in fact, it was one of the customers urinating on us from a great height. If only I had brought an umbrella I would have climbed the ladder and sought my revenge. Instead we threw some buckets of water over the topsides, and prepared to leave harbour as soon as possible.

8 September 1977: Passage from Le Palais to St Evette

0300 hours. We departed from harbour under engine in good conditions, tacking into a Force 3 but feeling cheated of the remainder of our night's sleep.

0730 hours: I took a fix from Ile De Groix-Pointe des Poulains. Not long afterwards we were treated to a truly majestic sight of dolphins migrating northwards in huge numbers, being chased by a magnificent killer whale which came along side us within a few feet, and remained there for a few minutes. The incident has remained one of my cherished memories of the cruise.

Not long afterwards Mary complained of feeling unwell, and by the time we arrived at the St Evette anchorage, she needed some advice from a pharmacist or doctor, and we had to replenish our fuel. She livened up after walking in the fresh air, so we returned to the boat carrying the heavy jerry can of petrol. Mary's problem turned out to be caused by a blockage in the exhaust system, resulting from emulsion formed by seawater mixing with the two-stroke oil, and the escape of carbon monoxide into the cabin.

A certain amount of panic was setting in, not only because Mary had been unwell, but because we had missed the critical time to make the passage through the formidable race at the Pointe du Raz, which runs at over ten knots.

Late in the afternoon we set off to find a boatyard at Tréboul where we could leave *Espinet 2* for the winter if we were unable to force our way through the Raz de Sein and ran out of time to make the passage back directly to Plymouth. This would be a very costly business, but on the other hand it would be very embarrassing to be absent for the first day of the school year, as I had been caught out at sea on several occasions, and had quite often been late for work as a result.

Passage from St Evette anchorage to Plymouth or Tréboul.

As we approached the Raz de Sein the tide was getting stronger all the time, and our progress was minimal, so we started to motor sail and tack into the head wind. No matter how hard we tried we could not reach the critical point at the bottleneck, where the foul tide was acting like a brick wall. My absolutely last option was to sail very close to the 'Razor's Edge', where the rocks slow down the currents.

This called for nerves of steel, and a constant watch of the depth meter. As we sailed towards the very edge of the razor, we had a riding turn on the main winch. If we turned downwind away from the dangerous rocks, the boat would be swept away back towards our starting point, which would lose us the tide, and make it impossible for us to sail back home this year. Stan was scared out of his wits seeing us hurtle towards the rocks at nine knots. Mary, on the other  hand, took the helm while I freed the rope just in time to turn the corner into slacker water. What a wonderful example of Mary's courage in the face of obvious danger!

Figure 39 shows La Pointe du Raz in fine weather and does little to convey the danger we faced in the hell hole of the race. Our course started at the top left-hand corner of the photo, and it followed the coast round the headland into the Bay of Douarnenez. We sailed in and out of the off-lying rocks, where the currents were weaker, until we were out of reach of the race. It was interesting to learn that the race is so powerful that it can flatten seas caused by the greatest storms.

During the evening the wind died away, leaving us with not

Figure 39   La Pointe du Raz.

enough fuel to reach Tréboul, so we arrived at the marina in the dark, having been delayed by the need to refuel. Imagine our surprise to find a crowd had gathered to meet us, because our efforts to force our way though the race had been reported, and the lifeboat crew had been on standby, because of their concerns for our safety. Everybody was anxious to learn why we had attempted to force our way through the race against a spring tide, and against a head wind. They were also curious to learn where we had come from, and why we were in such a hurry to get home. They were impressed to find that we had sailed over a thousand miles, and had crossed the Bay of Biscay twice.

From that moment onwards we received nothing but kindness, friendship, and above all the practical help in solving our problems. One of the club members offered us accommodation, and the manager of the boat yard took care of *Espinet*'s winter storage and gave me permission to use the yard's facilities for the Easter refit. Another member found a kind taxi driver who was prepared to give

137

up his Sunday to drive us to Roscoff to catch the last Brittany ferry back in time for the start of the new term. All these generous and hospitable club members made the three of us feel very much at home.

We had just enough time left to gather all our personal effects and some valuable gear, which we put in large see-through sail bags, and we were on our way, with the driver's foot firmly on the accelerator for ninety nine per cent of the journey to the ferry terminal. We made it with barely enough time to thank our driver and pay him for his trouble.

The ferry docked at Millbay dock next morning, where we joined a queue for customs clearance, together with all our large see-through sail bags. We were made to wait until everyone else had been checked before the staff set about rummaging though all our dirty washing and clutter, smiling at our embarrassment.

It was a frantic dash to my creek-side cottage to change my clothes and my persona, ready for the start of the first day of the school year. It is such an important occasion that all the staff are expected to be on duty, and there would be no excuse for lateness. It was a deeply tanned 'sailor at heart' who arrived just in time for assembly, and still walking on his sea legs. The entire teaching staff had arrived early, and no doubt had been wondering what had happened to me at sea.

During the mundane routine of the assembly, my mind began to contemplate how I was going to refit *Espinet 2* for the next year, and when I could return her to the Tamar mooring. I decided to spend the Easter break doing the refit and then potter about cruising with Mary, after spending some quality time with our new friends at Tréboul. We would return home via the Channel Islands. The assembly ended, and I came down to earth with a bump. The good times were over for another year!

17

Smuggling

I must own up to having sold my entire stock of duty-free cigarettes when I ran out of funds whilst sailing single-handed in France. However, most people I have known, have been guilty of minor infringements, and in France smuggling is regarded as a national sport, which should be enjoyed whenever possible.

In one of the small communities on the Brittany coast, the local boat owners, who were mainly fishermen, had been in the habit of buying their televisions, fridges, and other expensive goods in the Channel Islands, where shopping was so much cheaper. Each weekend the boats returned home at night laden with goodies, and the customs officer would be conveniently asleep. Unfortunately for the shoppers he was replaced by a younger officer, who started making comments about all the new television sets and other expensive items which appeared each week. The menfolk decided that something had to be done, or else their perks would cease.

To teach the officer a lesson, the men picked him up, turned him upside down, and then dropped him into the muddy waters of the creek. He climbed out of the creek covered from head to toe, in thick smelly mud. 'Let this be a lesson not to comment on our shopping habits,' he was told. Sometimes, however, custom officers genuinely fail to see what is going on under their noses, as the following incident illustrates.

One day my friend and his wife watched a boat anchor in the bay in front of their house. Two of the crew inflated a large and expensive rubber dinghy, which they promptly launched and rowed into the harbour, where they deflated it, packed it into its container and went on their way. Later in the day, to their surprise, our friends watched a repeat of the inflatable-dinghy incident. They did not understand why the dinghy never returned with its crew to the boat. The simple explanation was that smugglers had been delivering the expensive dinghies to their customers right under the noses of the customs officers.

In France there is a law which states that all customs officers must walk the entire length of the section of the coast which is allocated to them once a year to discharge their duty. Someone I knew lived at the end of one such section, and he was on good terms with the local customs man. By mutual agreement he would call in for a drink. His host would lift the seat of the long settle in which he stored his contraband spirits, and invite his guest to help himself to whatever he fancied. I wondered just how much contraband the officer closed his eyes to.

One of the locals owned his own aircraft, in which he made regular visits to the Channel Islands from a nearby small airport. It is a well-known habit of the French to stop work at midday, and then start again at two p.m. or at four p.m. during the heat of the summer. The pilot simply landed with his shopping when everybody was at home having lunch.

On one occasion I had the good fortune to discuss smuggling in the West Country with a customs and excise officer. He said that the service was not unduly concerned about small quantities of tobacco or alcohol being brought in by yachtsmen, but they always kept tabs on those whom they suspected of smuggling, in case they moved on to drugs and people smuggling.

When my family and I moved to the West Country, we stayed in a rented cottage which we had previously used as a holiday home. Naturally we explored every nook and cranny from Polperro to Looe, and we took an interest in the local history of smugglers and wreckers. There were two cafés close by, each of them close to its own small beach and its own small bay. The least popular of the two changed hands during our time at Talland. The new owners soon blended in with the locals. The wife made every effort to join in the social life of the community, and her husband was a very keen diver who kept his inflatable high speed dinghy in the car park.

Talland was a great place for my young family to be during the warm sunny days, but in the dark, winter, moonless nights, strange sounds excited their imaginations about the stories which they had heard, of smugglers and wreckers.

Without warning the police and customs and excise team raided the newcomers' café. A large quantity of cannabis was found hidden under the floorboards. The couple had imagined that they had found the ideal spot to set themselves up as professional smugglers, but unfortunately for them, the local gossip about strange noises down on the beach gave the game away, which led to the husband going directly to jail without collecting the two hundred pounds. No doubt he had plenty of time there to play Monopoly and Scrabble.

An airline pilot told me that he had been on a regular flight to Switzerland, and one day he decided to buy his wife a very expensive watch for her birthday present. He made up his mind that for the first time in his career he was not going to pay duty on his shopping. He calculated that the chances of being stopped were insignificant so he need not worry. He must have shown that he was ill at ease because he was stopped and searched.

He handed his overnight bag to the officer, then took off his gloves and put them on the table. Nothing was found, and he did not lose his job, because the tiny expensive watch was inside one of the gloves.

One late-night session in a country pub, I was chatted up by two of the locals, who seemed more than interested in my sailing and my yacht than I would have expected. Details of my trips abroad were of particular interest to these two characters. After they had plied me with several more drinks, I was propositioned as to hiring *Espinet 2* with myself as skipper to do a few trips to France. I was sober enough to read between the lines of their conversation, and realised I was being sounded out as to whether I was up to something illegal. Back in 1968 I was told that some locals were walking towards one of the secluded bays between Polruan and Polperro, when a number of foreign-looking men appeared on the path leading from the lonely beach, and each were carrying plastic bags full of their belongings, so I was already aware of the people smugglers operating in the area. Needless to say, I kept well away from that particular pub and those undesirable characters after that.

18

Easter 1978 and Time for Espinet 2's *Annual Refit*

I had planned to complete the refit with the help of my friend Alan, who had volunteered to overhaul the engine completely, so I was looking forward to having trouble-free motoring at last, without the fear of gassing the crew with carbon monoxide.

We set off on the Brittany ferry in strong gale conditions. At one stage the ferry was unable to recover from a broach, and it remained heeled over at an alarming angle for ages before it recovered. The captain had the good sense to change course to windward to stabilize the ferry. Once the passengers had calmed down I went to the lounge at the front of the ferry to see what the seas were like. Walking along the deserted passages, I met a man who was walking with difficulty, because he was leaning at an angle of forty degrees. No wonder I had been lurching all over the place without having touched alcohol! The sight I watched spellbound was awesome – each time the ferry buried her bows in the huge waves, they broke into massive cascades, which reached well above the height of the bridge. Eventually the ferry found some respite from the gale, in the lee of the Brittany coast, but even there we had to crawl along the coast towards Roscoff. However, our troubles were far from over, because docking was dangerous in such violent winds. The first two attempts ended as the wind drove the ferry sideways towards the danger buoy, but on the third attempt a small harbour boat came alongside to relay to the captain details of what exactly was going on. I was very relieved when we finally tied up, because another failure would have meant going back out to sea to ride out the storm.

Odette, our friend who had been so kind to us when we stayed with her at Douarnenez, had been waiting for us to arrive for all the extra hours we had been delayed. Thank goodness! Unfortunately she was unable to drive in the dark because of her very poor sight, so I had to cope with her car's poor headlights which were weaker than Toc H lamps, a gear shift which resembled a walking stick, driving on the wrong side of the road, being directed by someone who was not familiar with the route, and violent gusts of wind strong enough to shift a road roller. However, both Alan and I were very grateful for Odette braving the elements to collect us.

The weather did improve and our stay at Chez Odette was first class. We also struck lucky at the boat yard where we worked on the refit, as we soon made friends with a kindred soul who was working on his steel-hulled yacht. At regular intervals he plied us with cans of lager. It was strange to find that his mobile workshop was a vintage Merc, where he stored cans of paint, life jackets, and lots of boat paraphernalia. Towards the end of Alan's holiday, Alan suggested that we invite him to lunch, as a thank-you for his generous supply of lager. Our new friend was pleased with the invite, and offered to drive us to one of his favourite restaurants.

We were driven in his brand new Merc, which he parked out of sight, because the prices would be doubled if the restaurant owner saw us arrive in that. The meal was fabulous, our guest was on good form, and the cost was very modest. It made a very pleasant ending to Alan's visit to Tréboul. Our friend was embarrassed when I asked him where he lived, replying that he lived in a château, but its roof had many of its slates missing. I thought that his reply was a timely way of putting us at ease.

Mary was the next volunteer to give me a hand with the refit, and with her help *Espinet 2* was once again in pristine condition, and ready for collection at the beginning of the long summer holiday. We still had several days before we were due to return home, so now we could relax and chill out with our friends at the sailing club, where we were treated as adopted members of one big happy family.

One unfortunate incident occurred when a uniformed officer from customs and excise approached me. He told me that I had illegally imported my yacht, and I owed VAT on the current value of it. My heart stopped for a moment, as I realised that I was well and truly in the mire right up to my neck. My friends gathered round the unpopular man, and made it quite clear what they thought of his intervention. Whether they pleaded on my behalf, or perhaps threatened! I never knew, but the matter was never mentioned again. Mary and I could look forward to some quality time, sailing *Espinet 2* in the company of such friendly folk later in the season.

Completion of the Cruise from Plymouth to St Sebastien, Spain

The cruise started in 1977, and ended back at Plymouth on 4 September, 1978!

Mary and I returned to Tréboul to find *Espinet 2* with her mast stepped, looking well valeted, and moored at the main pontoon in the marina. It was not long before our sailing-club friends appeared and gave us a hearty welcome back into the fold. Mary's son Brian hitchhiked all the way from the South of France to join us sailing locally, and pottering about like laid-back tourists.

However, our first trip round the bay suddenly stopped when Brian went below to make us a cup of tea. 'I am up to my knees in water down here,' he said in his usual casual manner, which was typical of his style of humour. This was no joke, however. With a Force 6 blowing, a choppy sea, and five miles at least to get back to the marina, it was going to be a far more exciting trip than I had anticipated. Pumping like hell and bailing, we motor sailed as fast as possible to get back before we sank! The water was still well above the cabin floor when we moored up. The reason for the leak was caused by the drying out of some timber under the counter,

Figure 40   Mary's light reading.

which left a nasty gap in the planking. The following day I gathered all the bits and pieces needed to repair the leak, and then I inflated the dinghy. Just as I started leaning forward to fasten the dinghy in position, it tipped the entire contents into the water. Mary, who was in the cabin at the time, called out, 'What is going on, Brian?'

146

Figure 41   Charlie Brown and Odette.

'Don't worry, he is only going down for the third time,' he replied. When I fell into the drink I was smoking a cigarette, and the first thing I did was to throw it away still alight. Nobody has ever believed my story but I am still sticking to it. Perhaps you can imagine how I felt having lost all my tools and materials, as well as my somewhat deflated dignity.

We did manage to spend three days sailing locally. The first trip was with Charlie Brown the dog and Odette as our guests. The next

Figure 42   My new crew?

trip was with some young children, who were more interested in playing than sailing. The third trip was to take one of Odette's friends, who happened to live near me in Cornwall, round the whole of the Bay of Douarnenez. Odette suggested that we organise a party at the sailing club to repay our friends for the parties they had invited us to. She not only made sure it was a success, but gave us some tips on how to save some of our funds. Needless to say, everybody enjoyed themselves, but we were sad to be leaving our friends behind.

9 August 1978, 1130 hours: We left Tréboul bound for Camaret, and were touched by the noisy send-off we had from the crowd, who had gathered at the harbour mouth, armed with foghorns. We even had one of the Dragon Class yachts to escort us into the bay.

1755 hours: Dropped anchor in Camaret harbour. The weather had improved, and was going to remain settled. Things were looking good and we could expect to avoid any cyclonic storms, or even a modest gale during the remainder of our holiday.

10 August 1978: Passage from Camaret to L'Abervrach

1400 hours: Our late departure was timed to take advantage of a strong tide, to help us through the Channel du Four, which would ensure that we would reach our destination before dark. By the time we reached Corn Carhai Lighthouse the strange rock shapes and the bow section of the *Amoco Cadiz* looking skywards looked menacing. The pollution was everywhere. Strong currents pushed us towards Petit Pot de Beurre, but there are always strong currents along the coast of Brittany, as I have found out many times.

2045 hours: Picked up a buoy near L'Abervrach marina, and then I took some photos of *Espinet 2* bathed in glorious good weather sunset colours. We both slept well

11 August 1978: L'Abervrach to Roscoff

Gill, my eldest daughter, and her husband Jack had arranged to meet up with us at Roscoff for a few days pottering about in the Bay of Morlaix, and then visiting Morlaix and the old town of Roscoff. They both settled down to life on board, although Jack was ill at ease sailing in rough water and passing close to unmarked rocks. We locked into the Morlaix dock which lies at the head of a narrow river, and there are no safe places to moor until we reached the lock. This would mean that we had to rely on the engine to get us safely back to deep water in the bay when the time came for us to leave the dock. I spent far too much time trying to resolve the fuel-starvation problem, which did not go down well with the others, who were hoping to get out and about. I found Morlaix to be rather a dull town, so I was pleased when it was time to leave the dock.

149

No sooner had we left the lock than I sensed that the engine was going to play up just as we needed it most. Without wind I was obliged to lie flat on the cockpit floor and blow into the fuel tank to get enough pressure to force the fuel into the carburettor. The taste of two stroke still lingers in my memory to this day! All the way down the very narrow channel the engine continued to splutter and cut out, and with the lack of wind we had to rely on the ebb tide to keep us moving towards deeper water and light winds. Having experienced the hazards of the upper reaches of the Helford River the last thing I had wanted to do was to anchor in the river on an ebb tide. On our way downstream the crew of a passing yacht were amazed to see me applying artificial respiration to a non-existing body, and their laughter echoed down the valley, which rubbed salt into my wounded pride.

Fortunately there was enough wind for us to sail to the moorings near the old fort which featured in the TV series *Fort Boyard*. The moorings are situated in a dangerous spot, owing to conflicting currents. Picking up the buoy was very difficult for Jack because of the jerky motion of the boat and gusty winds. Needless to say, we all found it hard to sleep.

Fair weather returned for the trip back to Roscoff, where Jack and Gill boarded the Brittany ferry for their return journey back to Plymouth. It was such a pity that they both had to start work, instead of continuing with Mary and me to the Channel Islands, as they both were very much at home and had enjoyed the sailing.

15 August 1978: Passage from Roscoff to Perros-Guirec

After a late breakfast we lifted the anchor and set sail along the coast, hoping to meet up with Jean and Genevieve, whom we met in 1975 in St Peter Port. This time we locked into the marina at Perros-Guirec without having to anchor in the bay, and the weather was still fine and settled. As luck would have it, our friends arrived at the marina just after we did, having returned from one of their regular 'shopping trips' in the Channel Islands. Jean called out, 'We are off to a festival in an hour's time, so we hope that you will be ready for us to pick you up.' We enjoyed the traditional festival, which was held in a fascinating old countryside town. The town boasted three squares in which groups of bagpipers, drummers and dancers entertained the multitude of die-hard traditionalists. I found that the music and the dancing tends to put everyone into a trance. Afterwards we returned to our friends' delightful bay-side croft, where our social life continued in full swing until it was time to go. Alas! Again we were flushed out of the marina through the lock at an incredible rate, into the bay and on our way home via St Peter Port.

17 August 1978: Passage from Perros-Guirec to St Peter Port, Guernsey

The only incident on this trip was passing through a riptide near the southern approach to St Peter Port, when I had to change course very quickly to avoid a deep whirlpool. The only other place where I have seen one is at Devil's Point on the lower reaches of the river Tamar.

Our stopover in the St Peter Port marina for essential supplies of duty-free spirits and fuel was all too brief, so we treated ourselves to one last drink and a snack before sailing. I ordered two large pastis (meaning Pernod), to which the waiter replied, 'We don't serve those, but we have sausage rolls.'

Our continental holiday was all but over, and we would soon lose our freedom of the seas.

19 August 1978: Passage from St Peter Port to Plymouth. Channel Crossing

Our planned course was to make for Salcombe, and depending on the weather we might stay there, or continue on to the Barbican dock for customs clearance. Head winds, poor visibility, constantly changing tack every two hours, and being vigilant about listening for the sounds of shipping – all these were very tiring. The lack of a direction finder always makes for uncertainty about dead-reckoning navigation, and it was not easy to reassure Mary as to where we were going, and she could not see why we had to change direction so often.

Eight miles south-east of Start Point, we met disturbed seas which shook the wind out of the sails, and having only a few pints of fuel left, we were at the mercy of the weak and contrary winds. Gradually the wind settled and strengthened, so I decided to take advantage of it, and we headed directly for Plymouth with the genoa still set. The wind continued to harden and we pressed ahead.

By the time we rounded the Great Mew Stone we were seriously over-canvased, but I was enjoying the thrill of overtaking every other yacht in sight. We headed towards Drake's Island, where I planned to drop the large sail in the lee of the island, because the gale-force wind was too strong for Mary to manhandle the sail below. I told her to take the helm instead. This required every ounce of her strength to keep on course, because the boat was so unbalanced with just the mainsail set. The engine had already given up the ghost, which left me to sail into the Barbican under mainsail only, weaving in and out of the different boats, whose skippers were all desperately seeking shelter with little regard for anyone else. Panic was almost tangible except on board *Espinet 2*, where Mary once again excelled in helping me cope with very difficult conditions, and she surprised some of the crews with her casual manner under adversity. She dropped the mainsail just at the right moment, and we came alongside the quay at a snail's pace, which was just as well because there was not a drop of fuel to get the engine going, to enable us to manoeuvre through the log jam of boats to reach the safety of the quayside.

Customs House was closed, and the obligatory phone call failed to produce the duty officer. We waited endlessly with a tantalizing smell of fish and chips torturing our empty stomachs. Mary could endure her hunger no longer, and followed her nose to the place of torment. She returned wiping her mouth, and carrying the remains of two large portions of fish and chips.

I in the meantime was being given the third degree by a bad-tempered customs officer, who had been called away from his weekend break to give us clearance. He was very suspicious to find Mary had left the boat illegally, and promptly turned everything upside down in his hunt for any contraband, but he failed to find the only bottle of wine, thank goodness!

We arrived at the mooring on the river Lyner only to find that it had been poached, so I was obliged to drop anchor and leave *Espinet 2* for two days being buffeted by a strong gale. I fretted over her safety, and made numerous visits to make sure she had not dragged her anchor.

The grand total mileage for the extended cruise to Spain and back was over one thousand five hundred miles, which did not include incidental day sailing. My thanks go to Mary for helping me realise my ambition to cross Biscay twice, and to my son Paul, together with all those friends Mary and I made en route.

19

The Water Spout

Mary and I had promised her friends Peter and Marion that we would take them on a short cruise in the West Country, but it had been difficult to arrange because of conflicting commitments. Eventually we agreed a date, which unfortunately coincided with a huge depression which covered the whole of England and Wales, except for Torbay and Plymouth. These areas were due to have moderate conditions, so I decided to go ahead with our planned mini-cruise, rather than disappointing our guests, but on no account would I go outside the area of moderate weather.

All went well and we enjoyed our visits to Salcombe, Dartmouth, Brixham and Torquay, with the exception of the problem of ferrying the four of us back to *Espinet 2*, which was anchored in the middle of Brixham harbour. The four-man rubber dinghy had developed a leak in its floor. We were obliged to bale out with a baked bean tin, paddle like hell, and pray we would reach *Espinet 2* before we sank. The water level kept on rising as the pitch of Mary's voice intoned my disgrace at owning a leaking dinghy. Marion, who was slightly more sober than the rest of us, managed to hail a passing motorised dinghy by shouting, 'We are sinking,' and the owner kindly escorted us back to our boat. We must have looked and behaved like four young children playing in a kiddies' plastic paddling pool. The next day we tied up alongside the quay at Torquay to avoid using the leaking dinghy.

As we left the harbour bound for Dartmouth, the sky over the land was nutty slack black, but further out to sea the sky was clear, with a thin layer of clouds. The sun was visible through the thin

154

Figure 43   Brixham.

Figure 44   The daily paper.

Figure 45   The black cloud – Torquay.

Figure 46   Avoiding the tornado.

cloud, and had a corona around it. These rings of dark colours are a sign of bad weather, and the dramatic contrast of black clouds and a clear sky confirmed that there was trouble ahead.

It looked as though we had been caught out, and would be trapped in Torbay or in the river Exe. This would be highly embarrassing for both Peter and me, because our return to work would be delayed. I certainly could not abandon my pride and joy, anchored in bad weather and so far away. I decided to make for Dartmouth. I hoped that Peter and Marion would not be too frightened by sailing in the strong wind and rough seas.

Having rounded Berry Head, we were passing Sharkham Point when I was horrified to see a huge water spout coming directly towards us from the Start Point direction. The safest option was to sail as fast as possible away from the coast and the advancing water spout. Grossly over-canvased and getting wetter every minute, we ploughed through the waves towards the open sea for some four miles, before the water spout collapsed. We did not know until the next day that the water spout caused the death of two sailors, when they were hit by the great pillar of water whilst sailing off Hope Cove.

Our long, slow progress beating to windward, and to Dartmouth, felt like riding a bucking bronco in a never-ending cloud burst. Even below deck it was hazardous when Marion tried to use the heads. Her unladylike language as she tried in vain to get out of her wet-weather gear was surpassed by her cries of frustration as she endeavoured to remain seated. Considering the fright level had been nearly off the scale, both our friends had coped remarkably well.

Our overnight stay in the marina at Dartmouth saw our spirits rise, and the weather improve dramatically. The sunshine, a fair wind, and an easy ride through the Start Point race made for a relaxed and pleasant passage back home. Peter was very pleased with himself, because he caught a 'meal for four' on the way back. We all enjoyed a superb fresh fish dinner and a fine Chablis. Our friends were no longer novices.

Dartmouth and the Royal Navy

Mary, Joe and I sailed to Dartmouth one summer's day, in fairly strong conditions, which I enjoy. *Espinet 2* made light work of powering through the Start Point race with all her light-weather canvas set. Right in the middle of the disturbed waters of the race, one of the jet-engine-propelled patrol boats called *Sabre* decided to show us our inferior position in the pecking order of boat owners. I could almost see the smirk on the coxswain's face as he opened the throttle and overtook us at high speed, and close enough to disturb our water. Fate dictated that we would meet the coxswain and some of the crew in the Chain Ferry pub in Dartmouth that evening.

Bill the coxswain recognised us and invited us to join his crowd for a round of drinks, by way of an apology for our close encounter. Several rounds later we were all invited on board *Sabre* for a nightcap. All went well for a while, until Joe started to lurch and sway towards the engine room. His glazed eyes were fixed on the fascinating instruments and a red warning notice which concerned the starting procedure for the jet engines. Bill promptly detailed a rating to stop him from starting up the engines or anything else.

Bill tried his hardest to get me drunk, but I had noticed that he had designs on Mary, so I kept relatively sober, as the last thing I wanted was to lose my first mate to the Royal Navy. Just before we abandoned his ship, he asked me for our sail number, and the time of our departure. Having been the butt of the Royal Navy's sense of humour before, I guessed that he obviously had some nasty practical joke in store for us if he could catch up with us somewhere on our way back to Plymouth. Prudently we agreed to leave earlier than we said, so that we could avoid playing dare in the Start Point race, or thwarting something equally unpleasant.

We had enjoyed our brush with the Royal Navy and Bill's sense of humour, which was typical of the Senior Service. I wondered if our paths would cross again. I also enjoyed the lively trip along the Devon coast in sunshine, and up the Tamar to my mooring near Brunel's iconic bridge.

Navy Days

Owning a boat does have its perks when it comes to watching the Navy Days from a hand-picked vantage point on the water, from one's own mobile apartment. It is like being in a Royal Box at some grand event. The previous year I had chosen to stay in the middle of Plymouth Sound in order to watch the activities on the water. We waited in vain for the ships to appear, when suddenly a Delta Wing Bomber targeted us, and did maximum rate turn just above us, at almost stalling speed. Its noisy engines nearly shattered our ear drums, and actually shook our bodies. The following year I chose to sail up the Hamoaze on the Cornish side, and anchor at the junction with the Lyner River. This should be an ideal spot for us, without interfering with the demonstrations. However, we were spotted by the dockyard Police, who chased us in their launch. One of the crew indicated that we should get lost. At the time we were sailing on a starboard tack, and the launch was the overtaking vessel. Clearly we had right of way, and I knew that we were doing nothing illegal. I replied with a suitable sign-language response. The launch pulled away from us like a scalded cat. We continued to our chosen vantage spot and waited for the first demonstration. Suddenly the sky above us was filled by a flight of helicopters playing tag, and then they dive bombed us one after another, as we had been their chosen target. Our world seemed to shake apart as the pilots invented manoeuvres which centred on *Espinet 2*.

I decided to move further downstream to a less noisy spot, but we had not gone far when we were confronted by *Sabre*. Bill the coxswain opened the throttle and started to jostle us in a menacing manner. It was obvious that he was trying to frighten the living daylights out of us. *Sabre* got nearer and nearer, and its engines stopped. Bill called out, 'I will see you later.' I greatly admired Bill's ability to call up reinforcements to sort me out for my cheek at taking on the Navy.

Sadly, Mary and I never did meet up with *Sabre* and her crew again. Soon afterwards we shared a drink or two with another fine

Royal Navy seaman, who was having his last drink in our local before sailing to the Falklands. I understand that he never returned. This one incident underlined what the role of these fine sailors is in times of conflict. I have always had a great admiration for the great sacrifices which they make in war and peace.

The River Dart and Sod's Law

Mary and I acquired the nicknames of Hyacinth and Richard. One does like to keep up appearances, even when one is sailing, especially on the river Dart, but one never knows when the best-laid plans dissolve into farce, just like they do on the TV sitcom, *Keeping Up Appearances.*

Approaching Dartmouth marina upstream on a spring ebb tide, I was hoping to make a professional job of berthing in a cul de sac. I turned across the current to enter the cul de sac, but at the worst possible moment the variable pitch propeller got stuck in neutral. In less than a second the strong ebb tide swept *Espinet 2* against a large cylindrical buoy, where she remained well and truly stuck. The crew tried their hardest to prise the boat free, as I tried to force the lever free with no success. Finally I managed to engage the forward gear, and we lurched forward towards the pontoon, picking up speed all the time. I was unable to find the reverse gear, leaving me with no other option but to go alongside a well-groomed and a very expensive yacht, with all our fenders placed to cushion the impact. The owner's wife had hysterics at the thought of having her boat and the pontoon cut in half.

Unbelievable but true, our fenders were so well placed just before the impact that no damage occurred, except to my pride, and to everone's nerves, especially the owner's. Richard and Hyacinth Bucket did not keep up appearances, but had good luck instead. All good sailors will at some time need good luck to survive.

20

The Magnet

1 August 1980: Passage from Saltash to St Peter Port, Guernsey

Alan and I had a few days free from commitments, the weather was settled and sunny, and it seemed a good idea to go sailing together. The forecast of NW Force 3, twelve-mile visibility, and a calm sea was ideal for a spinnaker run to St Peter Port, where Alan could rummage through the bric-à-brac and antique shops to his heart's content. At 1230 hours we set sail with the prospect of a trouble-free trip, ten gallons of fuel, and the opportunity for duty free to top up our wine stocks for the winter.

1700 hours: The wind in fact was barely SW Force 2, and our fuel was getting low as we had motor sailed for over four hours. It took seven more hours to cover the next twenty miles, with only a breath of wind, and the occasional burst of engine power to get us out of dead calm patches, before we sighted a lighthouse through the mist.

We now barely had enough fuel for docking purposes, if we could ever reach our destination, but it took a further half an hour to get close enough to identify the lighthouse. It was Les Hanois instead of the Casquets!!! What had gone wrong with my dead-reckoning navigation, because this was the most serious error I had made in my time at sea. We were now stuck with an almost empty fuel tank, in the wrong place, and in very poor visibility.

1435 hours: The wind had changed from NE 1–2 to NW 3–4 in a very short time, as we sailed towards the Little Russel channel. My experience told me that there would be a full-blown gale before we reached harbour. I noticed at one stage that the tide was setting in a

Figure 47   Alan without his magnet, 1 August 1998.

different direction to the one indicated in the tidal atlas. This did little to help my self-confidence, and sailing at over eight knots down the Little Russel, in very poor visibility and in rough water was becoming a nightmare. Reaching the safety of the outer harbour at St Peter Port was a great relief, and our first cup of tea tasted like nectar of the gods.

The reason for making the wrong landfall was quite simple. Alan was an antique dealer and was in the habit of keeping a small magnet in his pocket for testing metal objects to make sure they were non-ferrous. He had spent fourteen hours at the helm with his magnet still in his trouser pocket. We remained stormbound in the marina for four days, which gave us time to relax and enjoy ourselves. Alan had a great time scouring the bric-à-brac and antique shops, where he no doubt put his magnet to better use.

Before we left for the Channel Islands I remembered to tell Mary the time of our expected arrival, and that I would telephone her when we had arrived. Naturally she was alarmed when there was no telephone call for many hours after the deadline. She wisely called the coastguard, who told her that we had not arrived at the marina as planned. Mary was very pleased to hear eventually that all was well, but she could not understand how my navigation could be so bad that we almost missed the island.

Our return to Saltash was pleasant and uneventful, and we made our landfall spot on.

Note. Always check that there are no metal objects near the compass when sailing. Stainless-steel pots and pans left on the work surface, in the galley and beneath the compass can cause it to deviate.

Fuel Starvation and Its Medical Cure – a Catheter!

Readers will by now have noted that *Espinet 2* had a serious problem with its fuel supply. Alan produced a catheter and he suggested that I took it with Mary and myself when we set off for a day trip to Fowey and back. The idea was to use it to pressurise the fuel tank to keep the fuel running into the carburettor. The journey along the Cornish coast was like sailing down memory lane, with my dearest Mary beside me. What more could I possibly want on a sunny day, apart from an engine that did not keep stopping?

As soon as we started to sail home, the wind died away, so I tried to start the engine but it refused to cooperate. Mary produced the catheter which 'did just what it said on the label', providing someone kept squeezing the rubber balloon. Fearing that Mary would sue me for repetitive strain injury, I reluctantly swapped jobs from time to time. We reached Rame Head just as the engine spluttered to a halt. It was a very, very slow job coaxing *Espinet 2* back to her moorings with only a suggestion of wind to help us.

My frustration with my troublesome engine reached breaking point. I vowed that I would not put to sea again, until the problem was resolved. The petrol tank had been installed just beneath the cockpit floor, and there was insufficient height between the fuel level in the tank and the carburettor to make the engine work when the tank was low. Alan promised to cure this problem, as long as I could clear the blockage in the system.

Just to reach the petrol tap and filter, which was underneath the tank, I had to contort my body so much it was agonising. I emptied the tank and then pushed a piece of metal into the hole, as I had done many times before to clear the blockage, but still no fuel appeared and I knew that the tank was not empty. I found a longer piece of metal and pushed it further into the tank, but this time something was definitely blocking the hole. Eureka! I had at last discovered a small gauze filter which was clogged with muck, and every time the tank was nearly empty the muck gathered around the gauze and finally stopped any fuel from reaching the engine. Alan was delighted with the good news, and promptly rushed to the nearest car breakers to buy an electrical petrol pump which he duly installed.

From that moment onwards, the engine always started at the push of the button, and never again did it let me down.

Sailing Backwards

Engine failure can be embarrassing, as I know to my cost, but I am not the only one who has been afflicted. A friend recounted an incident which happened when he was delivering a large vintage yacht, which had just been restored and was in first-class condition. He was due to deliver this fine vessel to a small harbour in Brittany, and he had more than enough competent, able-bodied crew members who wanted to run the boat, which left Tom the skipper with very little to do. As they approached the harbour, however, he took command because he wanted to make a good impression on the locals. The sails were dropped and bagged, the mainsail had its cover on, and all the necessary ropes, sheets and fenders were put in their proper place. Tom pressed the start button and the engine remained lifeless. He tried again. Alas! the engine was dead. He darted below and found that the starter motor was submerged in the bilge water.

Meanwhile the flood tide was taking them nearer the harbour, where the local primary teacher had her class of excitable kids gathered round her on the quayside, as she explained how the sailing boats worked.

Tom had the presence of mind to turn the boat back to front, and use the tide and the tiller to bring it alongside. At the very moment they tied up, one of the little darlings said, 'Please miss, I thought that all boats went with the sharp end pointing forward.'

Tom seized the initiative, and asked the attractive young teacher to join him for a meal on board, where he would be happy to explain what goes on. She accepted the invitation, but knowing Tom, I imagine they did not waste their time talking about sailing.

Espinet's Engine Fails with Tom Onboard – How Embarrassing!

Not long after I had become familiar with my new twenty-two-foot prototype half-ton class yacht, I decided to invite Tom for an evening sail, as he had shown an interest in my new toy. Unfortunately an easterly gale had made the conditions in Looe Bay very rough, but knowing that he had competed in a Round Britain race, I was sure that he would enjoy an hour of so toughing it out with me. We went ahead with our trip.

There was a strong flood tide, and a gale blowing directly up the river, which meant using the engine to get us out of the harbour. We managed to get halfway down the Banjo Pier when the engine died, so I turned round and let the tide and wind take us back to where we had started from. The engine refused to start for some obscure reason. Tom said, 'Why bother with it when we came to go sailing.'

I rose to the challenge, which was almost impossible. To reach the open water it would be necessary to tack all the way down to the end of the pier, and the river was far too narrow. Each time we

Figure 48   Looe, Cornwall, 1995.

tacked across the river, the wind and tide pushed us back upstream, but as we turned into the wind I kept as close as possible to the river bank or the pier, so we made progress in the slack water. As we approached the end of the pier *Espinet* was heeled over at least forty-five degrees, and half of the mast was leaning over the end of the pier. Having cleared the pier by a gnat's whisker, Tom took the helm, and I had the opportunity to watch him drive the boat through some man-sized waves. The impromptu trial had been just great.

165

21

Moving House, 1980

Mary and I decided to move from our bijou creekside cottage just a few yards further along the quay, to the steward's house of the Manor Sanctuary, with its old coach house and orchard. The vast amount of work required in renovating one of the oldest properties in Cornwall left us with less time for sailing. Extended cruises were out of the question, so I followed some sound advice which Alan Pape gave me one day. 'Never keep a boat swinging on her mooring, if you can't find time to sail her.'

Mary and I continued to sail whenever possible, but the time came when I could not justify the expense, because all of my disposable income was going into my new property. With a sad heart and an empty wallet, I sold *Espinet 2* in 1983.

The year before, Mary and I had arranged to swap houses with someone we had met on our travels, in the sailing club at Tréboul.

July 1983

Mary and I drove to Nice with two friends who lived five doors away. My friend Alan joined our party, in the middle of our seven weeks' holiday. It turned out to be a life-changing event, because Mary, Alan and I started considering moving to the south of France permanently.

It took five weeks of serious house hunting before we found a semi-derelict mas (an old manor house), which was an ideal project for us to renovate. It brought an end to my sailing, but heralded

166

the beginning of the happiest time of my life. Alan, Mary and I, sold up our properties and moved all our possessions, including two dogs, to our new home, which had no toilet facilities, twenty-eight leaks in the roof, no glass in the second-floor windows, and only one enormous front-door key which could not be copied. The story of our time in France, we have been told, would be a bestseller! I only hope that Mary and I will have time to write it one day.

A State Occasion

I had often thought that my sailing days were over before I moved to France, but I had plenty of opportunities to admire all the wonderful sailing boats in the Italian, French and Spanish harbours. Our time in France was eventually blighted by the death of Alan. Mary and I then bought a property back in the UK which we shared, but we found it very hard trying to settle in an urban environment which lacked the mountains and the wild countryside, and also the happy, polite and tolerant people.

My son Paul telephoned me one day in 1996 to ask me if I would like a trip up the Thames on board *Rona 2*, as he was due to deliver this fine ketch to the dock next to Tower Bridge, where she would be part of a promotional event for the London Sailing Project. Paul was the project manager. Naturally I jumped at the chance to go down memory lane, and visit the area where many of my father's ancestors lived, worked and sailed. Some of them sailed to distant lands, on the other side of the Atlantic, in their square-rigged vessels. One of these master mariners died in New Mexico, leaving his first mate to take his ship back home, together with the news of his skipper's demise.

My father worked for the Port of London Authority, and was based at the Surrey commercial docks when he retired from his job as quartermaster on many of the large passenger liners. I spent many happy hours watching the large vessels docking under my

Figure 49   The Thames waterside.

father's watchful eyes, and being spoilt by the pier head staff, and the landlady of the local public house.

What exciting memories came flooding back as *Rona 2* made her way up the Thames – memories of trips on paddle steamers to foreign places like Southend and Margate, eating my sandwiches on a tug as it dropped off the barges it was towing, leaving a solitary lighter man to guide his barge with only a large sweep (oar) to a muddy berth. I remember being awestruck by the skill of 'one man and his boy', tacking in the fast-flowing river, and sailing their Thames barge as nonchalantly as a crew sailing a mirror dinghy. The thought of putting an engine in these fine boats would have been frowned on by the watermen.

Dad had a great love of the sea, and he took every opportunity to get me out on the water, even if it was only the Woolwich free ferry, where he would take me below to see the highly polished engines driving the great paddles. Never could he nor I have imagined that my son would one day walk the decks of the world's largest square-rigged vessels, and become a well-known figure on the Thames.

168

With Paul as skipper and two river policemen as crew, we left the old Millwall dock, bound for Tower Bridge. The first landmark was the Royal Naval Hospital, where one of my mother's ancestors, Captain Dansay, became its Lieutenant Governor.

On the hill above the World Heritage Site was the Royal Observatory where I often crossed the Greenwich meridian, slid down the hill on make-shift toboggans on cold winter days, while Wolf stared down from his monument at the Thames and the magnificent panorama of the City of London. I recalled the *Cutty Sark* being rigged with miles of rope made locally, the workers looking more like apes as they swarmed all over the spars and ropes. My father's sea-faring ancestors lived on the Ballast Quay, next door to *Gypsy Moth* and *Cutty Sark*. They would have been very proud to have such famous neighbours. The recent fire which burnt out much of the icon of tall ships saddened the nation.

I recognised some parts of the riverside paths, but the Millennium Dome had replaced the gas works at Blackwall, and the Surrey commercial docks no longer existed. Much of the riverside further upstream had changed so much I had to ask the senior river policeman what had become of my memories. My countless questions about their river were answered with patience.

I had enjoyed every moment of the trip, and at times I felt my dad was standing beside me, especially as we approached Tower Bridge. To my surprise the bridge opened for us, which was strange because we had no reason to go beyond. We were the only vessel in sight and suddenly a multi-gun salute was fired from the Tower of London. The crowds of people standing on the bridge all looked to see which important person on board was being given a welcome which must surely usually be reserved for a Head of State.

Paul had skippered the Ocean Youth Club's London-based ketch, and with his local knowledge and contacts, he had been able to time our arrival to coincide with the opening of Parliament and the traditional gun salute!

I would like to think that my treat had been a pay back, for me spending so much of his childhood and his youth trying to drown

Figure 50   An OYC ketch.

Figure 51   Paul and me shooting the Ardèche rapids.

him. Watching him skilfully negotiate the narrow lock, I wondered if he had ever imagined when he sailed my two-man fishing lugger that he would one day walk the decks of famous sailing boats.

I have fond memories of my last sail.